DISCOVERING
WES MOORE

DISCOVERING
WES MOORE

WES MOORE

EMBER

Text copyright © 2012 by Wes Moore
Cover photograph courtesy of The OWN Network

Visit us on the Web! randomhouse.com/teens

Educators and librarians, for a variety of teaching tools, visit us at
RHTeachersLibrarians.com

The Library of Congress has cataloged the hardcover edition of this work as follows:
Moore, Wes.
Discovering Wes Moore / by Wes Moore.   p. cm.
ISBN 978-0-385-74167-5 (trade) — ISBN 978-0-375-99018-2 (lib. bdg.)
ISBN 978-0-375-98670-3 (ebook)
1. Moore, Wes, 1978-—Childhood and youth. 2. Moore, Wes, 1975-—Childhood and
youth. 3. African American men—Biography. 4. Youth—Conduct of life. 5. African
Americans—Maryland—Baltimore—Social conditions—20th century. 6. African
Americans—Bronx (New York, N.Y.)—Social conditions—20th century. 7. Criminals—
Maryland—Baltimore—Biography. 8. Soldiers—United States—Biography. 9. Bronx
(New York, N.Y.)—Biography. 10. Baltimore (Maryland)—Biography.   I. Title.
F189.B153M65 2012   975.2'6043092—dc23   [B]   2011049135

ISBN 978-0-385-74168-2 (tr. pbk.)

RL: 5.9

Printed in the United States of America
10 9 8 7 6 5
First Ember Edition 2013

This book is dedicated to
my daughter, Mia,
who has added to my life
not only direction, but purpose.
I promise to dance with you always.

Contents

DISCOVERING
WES MOORE

A NOTE FROM THE AUTHOR

Writing this book has not been easy. It has forced me to accept a lot about my past that was not easy to accept, and to share a lot of my past that I had no intention to. I am not proud of many of the mistakes I made—some of which you will read about in this book—but I have a feeling I am not alone. I am excited about sharing this journey with you in the hope that you will see similarities between your experiences and mine. More importantly, though, I hope that you will see similarities between yourself and those around you. It's amazing how thin that line can sometimes be between our life and someone else's.

Growing up, I often felt as though I was on my own. I thought my decisions didn't have consequences and my opinions didn't matter to anyone but me. I was taught the difference between right and wrong, but I didn't fully understand it. Becoming an adult seemed like a constant struggle:

Do I do what I want or do what I'm told? Do I do what I know is right or do what all my friends are doing? Maybe, like me, you have been pressured by people you considered your friends to do things that got you in trouble. Maybe, in an attempt to be surrounded by others, you found yourself more alone than ever. It's a painful place to be. I get it. Fortunately, I came to understand that not only was I not alone, but I didn't have to be in that place forever.

When my first book, *The Other Wes Moore*, came out, people from all over the country and even the world picked it up and told me they liked it because they related to the stories. I was very happy about that. But I also knew that I wanted to do something for young adults, the young men and women who sit where I sat not long ago. I wanted to speak to the young people who are wrestling with the same fears, who are experiencing the same first love, who are trying to figure out in their own time and on their own terms what their journey to adulthood will look like. I particularly wanted to help that young adult who is on the brink of an important decision. One step can determine what a person's tomorrow will look like; I wanted to help make sure that step was the right one. I didn't fully understand until I was older how our choices can shape the rest of our lives. When I finally woke up to the truth, it was almost too late.

In these pages you will hear about my path and about that of another man, also named Wes Moore, with whom I have become close. A man who, like me, longed to learn what was right and to achieve a sense of belonging, a sense of acceptance. At times he succeeded; at times he fell woefully short. But at every juncture, he kept searching. You will read not only about the choices Wes and I made, but also about the people in our lives who helped us make those choices. Even when we didn't realize it, we were never alone. There were family, friends, coaches, teachers, and neighborhood role models who helped shape us, guide us, and protect us. And that was the key. Yet even though these people could act as advisors, ultimately, Wes and I had to decide whether to listen, to work, to fight, and to forgive.

I ended up receiving a prestigious scholarship to graduate school, serving in the army as an officer, and becoming a bestselling author. The other Wes Moore ended up being arrested and tried for felony murder. Around the time I was heading to England on a Rhodes Scholarship, the other Wes Moore was preparing to serve his prison sentence of life with no parole. You can get that much by reading the book flap or doing a simple Internet search. But that's not where the story starts, or ends. The chilling truth is that his story could have been mine, and the tragedy is that my story could have been his.

We all have stories to tell, important ones that need to be acknowledged, respected, and understood. Each story is a piece of the mosaic that makes a community; each community is in turn a part of our nation and our world. And as members of a community, we must remember that it is our responsibility to help people who might not have the support we have.

This book is not meant to congratulate or to cast judgment, nor is it meant to elicit sympathy. I simply want people to realize that they can find not just inspiration but understanding in the most unexpected places. I want people to know that one choice can lead to another life altogether. And finally, I want to show them that I wasn't as alone as I thought I was, and that maybe they are not alone either.

One
FOR KEEPS

Nikki and I were chasing each other around the living room. Every time she caught me I'd scream, but I loved every second. I was three. For every step her nine-year-old legs took, my little legs had to take four. It wasn't easy to catch up. Then, for the first time ever, I caught her in my grasp. But I had no idea what to do. So, in the spirit of three-year-old boys everywhere who've run out of better ideas, I punched her, laughing hysterically. My mother had a radar for mischief. She walked into the room right as my swing connected with Nikki's arm.

"Get up to your damn room!" Her yell startled me. "I told you, don't you *ever* put your hands on a woman!"

My mother has hands that hit so hard you only have to feel them across your face once to know you don't want them striking there again. I darted up the stairs to my room before those hands could reach me. If I hid myself, maybe

I wouldn't get punished. I slammed the door shut behind me just as her voice reached the second floor. "And don't let me hear you slam that—" *Boom!* I stared at the closed door, knowing it would soon be flying open again. I sat there in silence in the middle of the tiny room I shared with my baby sister Shani. I wasn't even sure why I was in so much trouble.

"Joy, you can't get on him like that." My father's baritone voice drifted up through the thin floor. "He's only three. He won't even understand what he did wrong. You really think he knows what a woman beater is?" It wasn't his style to yell. He stood six foot two, and he was thin, with a bushy mustache and a neatly trimmed Afro.

"Wes, he needs to learn what is good behavior and what is not!" my mom responded.

I heard my father's gentle laugh. "Cursing at him isn't the most effective way of making that point."

My parents' words faded into the background as I stared out the window, which overlooked a street in our busy neighborhood. On the dresser by the window sat a framed picture of Nikki and me. Colorful beads capped her braids—a hairdo she shared with my mother—and large, black-framed eyeglasses covered half of her face. I sat on her lap with my arm wrapped around her neck, a goofy smile on my face.

My full name is Westley Watende Omari Moore. My first name, Westley, is my father's. As for my middle names, my father loved the sound and meaning of *watende*, a Shona word that means "revenge will not be sought." It fit with his gentle, forgiving spirit. My mother thought Watende sounded too big and complicated for a tiny baby. She wanted to call me Omari, which means "the highest." I'm not sure what was less complicated or soaring about that name, but they compromised by giving me both.

Nikki's real name is Joy, like my mom's, but at a young age she was nicknamed after Nikki Giovanni, my mom's favorite poet. Mom was inspired by Nikki Giovanni's feminine strength, and she wanted to teach my sisters and me about Giovanni's message of tender love and fierce revolution.

I spent nearly every waking moment near Nikki, following her around as we teased each other. I couldn't understand what boundary I had broken in our game. This wasn't really a *woman* I was punching, anyway. This was Nikki. She was a comrade. Our bond was so close it was like we were one being. I thought there was no risk of offending her.

Years would pass before I understood how that blow connected to my mom's past.

•   •   •

My mother, Joy, came to the United States at the age of three. She was born in Lowe River, in the farmlands of Jamaica. Quiet Lowe River was far away from the tourist attractions along the coast. My mother's grandparents, my great-grandparents, were called Mas Fred and Miss Ros. They lived on land that had belonged to our ancestors for generations. But my grandfather dreamed of studying theology in a university in America. When the family finally earned enough money, they moved to New York.

Settling into the Bronx took effort for Joy, but she jumped into the melting pot with both feet. She studied the kids at school like an anthropologist, quietly observing their accents and their style. She imitated voices she heard on the radio, tailoring her speech to fit her surroundings. The Jamaican word "irie" became "cool." "Constable" became "policeman." "Easy-nuh" became "chill out." The melodic fluidity of the Jamaican accent gave way to the crisper diction of American English.

Joy entered American University (AU) in Washington, D.C., in 1968. It was a year marked by change, excitement, and tragedy throughout the world. In America, people were protesting the Vietnam War and marching in the civil rights movement in the name of peace and desegregation. The nation was divided. When Dr. Martin Luther King Jr. was assassinated, American cities exploded in riots. The riots were about more than King's murder, though. They were about years of racial segregation and economic inequality that were reaching a breaking point. Being quiet was no longer an option. People took to the streets to express their rage. They were so overcome by feelings of frustration and hurt that they were burning down their own neighborhoods. In many areas, people in white neighborhoods blockaded their streets, trying to keep the damage within the poorer, black areas. By the time the riots stopped, our nation's inner cities stood eerily quiet. To this day there are parts of our country that have not fully recovered.

Joy was furious that America, the very country that offered her new opportunities, still had laws and traditions that allowed her, as an African American and a woman, to be treated like a second-class citizen. She found support with her friends and fellow students in a campus group called OASATAU, the Organization of African and African American Students at the American University. OASATAU encouraged AU's black students to take an active interest in national, international, and campus issues. Being around students with similar ideas raised my mother's awareness—and her standards. She didn't want to change to fit into the melting pot; she wanted to be accepted for who she was.

The treasurer of OASATAU was a junior named Bill. Two months after he and my mom met, they were engaged. Two years later, they married. Bill looked for work while Joy was a junior in college. They were both still trying to find their feet as adults, though, and being responsible for each other overwhelmed them. The love haze wore off sooner than they had expected. The same qualities that had made Bill so attractive as a college boyfriend—his free and rebellious spirit, his fierce contempt for "the Man"—made him completely unreliable as a husband. He had long been an occasional drug user, but now he started using drugs daily. Joy knew that free love and drug experimentation were part of being young in the 1970s, but she didn't like them being constants in her own home.

As the years passed, Joy kept hoping that Bill's use of alcohol and drugs would stop. She believed that her fantasy could come true—that she could change and save her man. When Nikki was born, Joy expected that Bill would be motivated to cope with his addictions and step up as a dad. But instead his addictions got worse, and the physical and emotional abuse he inflicted on Joy intensified dramatically.

One night, Bill came home higher than Joy had ever seen him.

"Wash the dishes!" he shouted. He was kicking doors and cabinets shut, slamming glasses down on the table.

"Shush," she pleaded, "you'll wake Nikki."

The more she shushed him, the more he hollered. He moved in on her so that the two of them stood face to face. He grabbed her shoulders and threw her down. She was sprawled on the floor in her blue American University sweatpants, in agony, and before she could sit up, he grabbed her T-shirt and hair and dragged her toward the kitchen. She screamed without fear of waking Nikki anymore. He hit her in the chest and stomach. She kicked and scratched at his hands. He dragged her more roughly across the floor until her head slammed against the doorjamb. He released his grip on her hair and once again bellowed, "Wash the dishes!" He stood over her with a contemptuous scowl on his face. That look was the last straw. His abuse and humiliation were ruining the happy life Joy wanted for her daughter. Her will gave her the strength to pull herself up from the floor. On top of the counter was a wooden block that held all the large, sharp knives in the kitchen. She pulled the biggest one out and angled the blade at his throat. Her voice was collected: "If you try that again, it will be the last thing you ever do."

Bill seemed to suddenly become sober. He backed out of the kitchen slowly, not taking his eyes from his wife's tearstained face, her determined stare. A month later, Joy and Nikki left Bill for good. My mom vowed to never let another man put his hands on her.

• • •

The voices downstairs stopped. Someone was heading up to speak to me. From the sound of the steps, it was my father. His walk was slow, heavy, and solid. My mother tended to move up the stairs in a sprint. He knocked lightly on the door and slowly turned the knob. He peeked in, half smiling. I knew that, at least for now, my beating would wait.

"Hey, Main Man, do you mind if I come in?"

I'm told that Dad had many nicknames for me. "Main Man" is the only one I remember. I nodded slowly without looking up. He had to duck to clear the low doorframe. As he sat on the bed, he picked me up and placed me on his lap. My anxiety melted away like butter. I could not have felt safer, more secure.

"Main Man, you just can't hit people, and particularly women. You must defend people, not fight them. Do you understand?"

I nodded. "Is Mommy mad at me?"

"No, Mommy loves you, just like I love you. She just wants you to do the right thing."

With tiny, resistant steps I followed my father downstairs to face my mother and Nikki. I tried to copy his walk. When I moved like him, I felt as if I could match his strength. I was his main man. He was my protector.

That is one of only two memories I have of my father.

The other is of watching him die.

● ● ●

Dad was his parents' only son. He was tall without being intimidating, and he had a deep voice. When he graduated from Bard College in 1971, he dreamed of being a TV reporter. He wanted to address injustices across the country and the world, and to make sure his fellow citizens were in the know. He wanted to make an impact as a voice of truth. After traveling across America as a reporter, he returned to Maryland to host his own public affairs radio show. And he needed to hire a new writing assistant.

That assistant's name was Joy.

Their work relationship quickly turned to love. My father was intensely attracted to this short woman with a broad smile, who mixed a steel backbone with Caribbean charm. And in Joy's eyes, Westley was the opposite of Bill—calm, reassuring, hardworking, and sober. Westley and Nikki adored each other. They might not have shared DNA, but their bond was unbreakable. My parents married in a small ceremony in Washington, D.C. I entered the world two years later. We became a family of five when Shani was born in 1980.

• • •

On April 15, 1982, my father ended his radio news broadcast on WMAL with his signature sign-off: "This is Wes Moore. Thanks again, and we'll talk next time." But keeping the cheer in his voice was a struggle. For the past twelve hours he'd been feeling ill. Breathing was a chore.

He came home after midnight, when my sisters and I were already asleep. After finishing dinner, his favorite meal of smothered lamb chops, he couldn't sleep. He took an aspirin, hoping it would ease his severe sore throat and fever.

Once the sun rose, he got out of bed. He threw on a tattered blue flannel shirt and a pair of worn blue jeans. He got in his red Volkswagen and drove himself to the hospital. My mother took Nikki to school and Shani and me to the babysitter's. Then she rushed to the emergency room. She was shocked by what she saw. Her husband was slouched over in the hospital bed. His eyelids were drooping and his head was flopping from side to side. The doctors didn't seem shocked at all. They said they couldn't find anything wrong; he just had a bad sore throat and needed to rest.

They released him, not suspecting that they would be seeing him again soon.

Near six o'clock that evening, my mother was in the

kitchen, holding Shani as she and Nikki cooked potato pancakes for dinner. I sat at the dining room table coloring in my clown coloring book. I was months away from my fourth birthday. I heard my father coming down the stairs. His steps were strangely slow—not that firm tread I was used to. I got up to greet him at the foot of the stairs so he'd pick me up.

Then there was a crash, and I saw his body sprawled across the floor at the foot of the stairs. He was trembling uncontrollably.

Then: another crash, this one from the kitchen. I didn't want to take my attention away from Dad, but I was so surprised I whirled around. After hearing my father's fall, my mother had dropped the sizzling cast-iron skillet on the floor. I turned breathlessly back to my father and saw him gasping for air, clutching his throat. Hardly any sound came from his mouth. His normally strong features sagged in exhaustion, as if he were fighting against something powerful and cruel.

Mommy pushed past me. "Nikki, call 911!"

Nikki rushed to the phone. I could hear her repeating again and again, "I don't know what county we're in." Shani sobbed in the background, adding to the crazed symphony.

My mother bent over my father, trying to give him CPR. Shani, still crying, was draped over her shoulder. And I just stood there, staring. Not knowing what to do.

"Wes, Nikki, go outside! Signal to the ambulance crew the second you see them so they know where to go!"

Nikki took my hand and led me out to wait. The dusk

was turning to darkness as the police and ambulance crews arrived minutes later. The street was quickly becoming packed with people, who were watching anxiously, but I felt deeply alone. My mind was racing, but at the same time it felt empty.

The EMTs placed my father onto a gurney and raced back out. The ambulance doors slammed shut. Mom loaded us into the car and followed the ambulance to the hospital. The air was full of noises—Shani crying and Nikki making goo-goo noises to try to calm her down, and the loud siren of the ambulance in front of us—but it felt as silent as a tomb. No talking. No questions.

The hospital was only five minutes from where we lived, but the ride seemed long. We were sent to the waiting area. Shani had quieted down and was playing with her shoe-strings, while Nikki clutched me on her lap.

An ER doctor walked toward us.

"Mrs. Moore, I'd like to speak with you in private, if I may."

"He's dead, isn't he?" my mother demanded.

"I am sorry. By the time he got here . . . he was gone," the doctor said. "We tried, we tried hard. I am so sorry."

Then my mother passed out.

Dad was dead five hours after having been released from the hospital with the simple instruction to "get some sleep." The same hospital was now preparing to send his body to the morgue. My father had entered seeking help. But his face was unshaven, his clothing disheveled, his name unfamiliar, his address not in a wealthy area. The hospital staff looked at him suspiciously, questioned whether his illness was even real, and basically told him to deal with it himself. Now my mother had to plan his funeral.

We found out that he had died from acute epiglottitis, a rare but treatable infection that causes the epiglottis to swell and cover the air passages to the lungs. Numbing my father's throat was the worst thing the doctors could have done. My father could no longer feel it closing. His body suffocated itself.

Of the three of us kids, our father's death struck Nikki the hardest. She had known him the longest, and she was the only one old enough to understand what was going on. And there was another reason: Bill, her biological father, changed when my father died. While Dad was alive, Bill supported Nikki financially and took the time to see her and talk to her. After Dad died, the calls, letters, and checks stopped coming. Bill had been competing with my father for Nikki's love. With Dad out of the picture, the threat was gone and Bill no longer made an effort. It was as if my sister lost two fathers that day.

For days after my father's death, the phone rang non-stop. People crowded into our home. His death had created a major stir in the journalistic community. He was young, talented, and admired. His colleagues turned up to pay their respects. I saw the pain on their faces without understanding it. If my father had "passed on," like so many people told me, where had he gone? I wanted him to be mine for keeps.

The funeral took place at the Fourteenth Street Baptist Church, the church where my parents had been married six years earlier. My uncle escorted us to the mahogany casket in the front of the altar to see my father's body one last time. Dad looked serene now, not like the last time I had stood next to him, when he'd lain at the bottom of the stairs. My uncle gently pulled my hand to signal it was time to go, but I resisted moving away.

On tiptoes, I peeked into the casket and asked, "Daddy, are you going to come with us?"

Two

COURTSIDE IN THE BRONX

For two years after my father's death, my mother slept on the living room couch. The neighborhood was getting dangerous; there had been break-ins in many of the houses around us. My mother said she slept downstairs to stand guard over her children. She wanted to be the first person a trespasser ran into upon entering the house. Sleeping in the living room also allowed her to avoid the bedroom she'd shared with my father, but no one mentioned that.

My mother still tortured herself with doubts about my father's death. Had she asked the right questions at the hospital? Should she have pushed the doctors harder for a clear diagnosis? Why hadn't she been able to save him with CPR? In her anxiety, she unfairly blamed herself.

People around us didn't think she was coping well with her husband's death. They thought she needed help, not just in raising her kids, but also in raising her spirits. She had gained some weight, and her eyes were always tired and distant. We were surrounded by her longtime friends from college and my uncles and aunts from both sides of the family, but their support wasn't enough.

Finally, swallowing back tears, she called her parents one morning.

"Mom, I want to stick it out in this home I bought with Westley, I really do. But I can't take it anymore, I can't do this alone." She took a deep breath. "So if it's still all right, I think we need to move up to New York, with you."

My grandmother was thrilled. Before she even answered my mother, she called out to my grandfather, "Joy and the kids are moving to the Bronx!"

Three weeks later, Nikki, Shani, and I stood outside our car, staring with disbelief at our now-empty home. This was it. We were actually leaving Maryland.

"All right, guys, load up!" my mother yelled cheerily as she slammed the trunk of our lime-green Ford Maverick. Even as a kid, I knew my mother's lightheartedness was a disguise. She didn't know what we were headed for any more than we did. She paused to take one final look at our house, the house she'd lived in for six years. It already felt like a past life.

My grandparents weren't strangers to me; they'd spent quite a bit of time with us in Maryland. They were both recently retired—my grandfather from the ministry and my grandmother from twenty-six years as an elementary school teacher in the Bronx. I was excited to live with them, because they spoiled us like crazy. But I hated the idea of moving away from my friends and leaving the only world I'd known.

On the drive, Mom reminisced about her childhood in New York City. My mind flashed to movies and pictures of New York that I'd seen. Its energy seemed electric to me.

"It's safe there." She smiled at me in the rearview mirror. "In all the time I lived in New York, I never experienced crime, violence, nothing. There's a real sense of community. Always someone to look out for you and give you a hot meal when you need it. And the zoo is only a couple minutes away from our house!"

But once we left the interstate, the feeling in the car shifted. As we navigated the burned-out landscape of the Bronx, it must have been clear to my mom that things had changed.

The Bronx was home to an extremely diverse population. Areas such as the Italian-immigrant-settled Country Club neighborhood were among the wealthiest in the city but were only minutes away from the poorest district in the nation. When my grandparents moved from Jamaica to the United States in the 1950s, the South Bronx had already begun its transformation from a mostly Jewish area to one dominated by blacks and Latinos. When my mother was growing up in the Bronx, the sense of family and community was strong, despite rising poverty levels. With every decade that had passed since she left the area, things had gotten worse. In 1977, when President Jimmy Carter visited the

South Bronx, he said it looked like a war zone. Now, seven years after his visit, my mother was moving back.

When my grandparents arrived in the United States, their first priority was to save enough money to buy a house, and they chose one on Paulding Avenue. America allowed them to create a life they'd never dreamed of in their home countries of Jamaica and Cuba. To them, a house was a commitment to being Americans.

Somehow, their three-bedroom home always managed to stretch itself when people were in need of a place to stay. There were always at least five people living in that house, and sometimes as many as nine. Conditions were tight. With our arrival that late summer day in 1984, we brought the number of inhabitants to seven.

My mother called out "Almost there!" just as we stopped at a red light at the corner of Paulding and Allerton Avenues. Outside our car window, we saw a woman in short shorts that showed off scaly, ashy legs. She stumbled forward, her right hand tightly gripping a wad of money. She was approaching a boy no older than sixteen. He was darting his head back and forth as if on the lookout for something. As the woman reached him, the light turned green and my mother quickly stepped on the gas. Even craning my neck to look backward, I didn't see how that scene ended. When I faced front once more, I could see the nervousness in my mother's eyes reflected in the rearview mirror. Moments later we arrived at our new home.

My mother switched off the radio and turned off the engine. I got out of the car and wandered down the street in front of the house. My attention was attracted by a telephone pole to which a picture of a young girl was taped. Signs saying WE LOVE YOU, APRIL and SEE YOU IN HEAVEN were taped around the picture, and stuffed animals were scattered on the ground. The whole thing gave me the creeps.

I walked up the stone stairs behind Nikki to see my grandparents waiting there. My grandmother stood in the doorway, her hair in a light Jheri curl and a big smile across her face. "Welcome home!" she bellowed to us in her Jamaican accent. She held me to her chest in a tight embrace.

My grandfather stood directly behind her, waiting his turn to greet us. He was a short man, no more than five feet six, but you immediately felt the strength of his presence in every room he entered. He was dark-skinned and had a muscular frame that made him seem much younger than he was. His mustache tickled my face as he hugged me and kissed my cheek.

Unloading the car, my mother murmured to my grandparents about the woman buying the drugs from the young boy.

"I never said it was the same here, baby," Grandma responded gently. I hovered around them, trying to look busy spinning a basketball on my finger so they wouldn't suspect I was eavesdropping. Quietly, my grandparents told my mother how drugs and violence had crept into the neighborhood, and it didn't seem as though they would go away soon. They also talked about something I'd never heard of before: crack.

When they noticed me listening, they stopped talking.

My grandmother smiled brightly and nudged us inside. When she went into the kitchen, I heard my grandfather finishing the conversation with my mother. He spoke in a serious but reassuring tone. The changes in the neighborhood were never going to alter his belief in the basic goodness of the community, he said. He was determined to stick it out and do his part to heal what was broken in the Bronx.

Then my grandmother returned with a large pot of codfish and ackee, the unofficial dish of Jamaica, and a pot of grits. She had spent days preparing the food in anticipation of our arrival. My grandfather had served as kitchen helper, deboning the light, salty fish and chopping up the onions and peppers while my grandmother seasoned and cooked the dish to perfection. It had the unmistakable taste of something homemade.

I stopped spinning the basketball and sat down to eat.

• • •

I quickly grew antsy in the Bronx. I missed my friends, my familiar neighborhood, even my tiny bedroom. To cure my restlessness, I headed out into my new streets. I had thought my mother's rules were strict, but soon I realized that my grandparents' were ten times worse. Grandma and Grandpa made it very clear that Paulding Avenue was their home and their rules would apply.

"Wes, when the streetlights go on, you are to be back

home, you understand?" My grandmother said it without menace, but from her voice I knew there was no room for argument. She was stating fact, not asking my opinion.

"If you hear any foolishness, you get yourself right home. Right away. I don't care if it's daylight." "Foolishness" was Grandma's word for gunfire. These were not Bronx rules, these were West Indian rules. They were the same ones my mother had lived under, and they now applied to me.

One of those rules was that all chores had to be done before we even thought about going outside to play.

"Can I go play basketball?" I asked after dinner one day.

"Chores?" my grandfather asked.

"Done."

My grandpa raised his eyebrow. "Go, play. But come right back!"

I took my time getting to the courts, finding my rhythm as I dribbled the ball down the concrete sidewalks. I didn't want to seem like a tourist, but I was soaking everything in. People looked me up and down. I glanced back, gave them a nod, and continued practicing my crossover dribble. People were everywhere! Sitting on the stoops, hanging out on street corners, calling from windows. The *boom-bap* of early hip-hop tumbled out of the apartment buildings and mixed with Spanish music blaring from boom boxes.

Then there were parts of the Bronx that looked post-apocalyptic. Whole blocks were abandoned and left to decay. Buildings were charred from fires. I didn't learn until later that drug dealers were still making use of those abandoned buildings—and that landlords often hired arsonists to burn them down for insurance money. Folks walked by with vacant eyes flickering, their heads nodding off. I learned later that their swollen hands were telltale signs of drug injections.

I finally arrived at the courts and saw a handful of guys playing three on three. They looked a little older than I was, or at least bigger. They were all better on the court, too. The red iron rims had no nets, and since there's no real give on rims, every shot ended as either a silent swish or a high-bouncing brick. I was intimidated, but I hung around to watch. I knew my deadline for going back to the house wasn't too far off.

I was practicing my lefty dribble next to the iron gate that surrounded the courts when one of the guys fell hard to the ground. He had been accidentally hit in the face while driving to the basket. Blood trickled from his mouth. He quickly walked off to get some water and clean his face. No foul was called. I would soon learn that calling fouls just wasn't done.

They were down a player. All at once, they were looking at me. I was the only person on the sidelines.

"You good to run?" one of the boys asked me.

I dug up whatever confidence I had, placed my basketball on the ground, and walked toward them. My oversize sneakers clopped on the asphalt like a pair of hooves. Each boy called out his name as I gave him a quick dap, an informal greeting of clasped hands and bumped chests.

"What's up. I'm Ozzie."

"What's going on. Deshawn."

I tried not to grin too hard. "I'm Wes."

From this first moment, I could tell there was something special about being on a Bronx court. The basketball court is a rare sanctuary, a meeting place for every kind of ball-player. You'd find the high school all-stars running circles around the overweight has-beens, guys who'd played above the rim years ago and now were just trying to catch their breath. You'd find the drug dealers there, mostly playing the sidelines, betting major money on pickup games and amateur tournaments but occasionally stepping onto the court, smelling like a fresh haircut and wearing gear that was too fine to sweat in. But even they couldn't resist getting a little run in—and God help you if you played them too hard, or stepped on their brand-new Nike Air Force Ones.

You'd find the scrubs talking smack a mile a minute and the church boys who didn't even bother changing out of their pointy shoes and button-up shirts. You'd find the thugs pushing off for rebounds, and the A students quietly showing off silky jump shots and then running back downcourt with their eyes on the ground, trying not to look too pleased with themselves. There would be the dude sweating through his post office uniform when he should've been delivering mail, and the brother who'd just come back from doing a bid in jail—you could tell by his chiseled arms and intense stare, and the cautious smile he offered every time a passing car would honk and the driver yell out his name, welcoming him home.

We were all enclosed by the same fence, bumping into

one another, fighting, celebrating. Showing one another our best and worst, revealing ourselves—even our cruelty and crimes—as if that fence had created a circle of trust. A brotherhood.

I played hard, lost pretty bad, and loved every second. These kids were different from my friends in Maryland. They had swagger I'd never seen. I wanted to pick up on their lingo and style. I was glad to be their new teammate and I hoped we'd be friends.

We played until the streetlights switched on, my signal to head home. "When you playing next?" I asked, my confidence settling in.

"We'll be here tomorrow, same time," Deshawn said.

"Then so will I."

Three
THE CHAMELEON

My mother decided I was not going to a Bronx public school. She wasn't a snob, she was scared. The schools she'd grown up around were still there, but they were not the same places anymore. The buildings were a heap of crumbling walls and chipped paint. Even if you were among the lucky 50 percent who made it out in four years, there was no guarantee you'd be prepared for college or a job. Things were falling apart inside, as they were out in the streets. The halls of school were no safe harbor from the chaos outside.

No matter how much the neighborhood around us seemed ready to rot, my mother was determined to see us through. Since we'd arrived in New York, she had been juggling jobs to help provide for us three kids and her parents, doing anything from freelance writing for magazines and television to acting as a furrier's assistant. She would wake us up in the morning for school, and before we had finished getting dressed, she was off to work. At night, my grand-parents prepared dinner for the family and got us to bed. Mom would come in from her last job late and walk straight to our rooms, pull the covers tight around us, and give us our kiss good night. The smell of her perfume would wake me as soon as she walked in, and then comfort me back to sleep.

The school Mom wanted us to attend was Riverdale Country School. Riverdale was as big as a college campus. It had manicured lawns, and buildings covered with ivy. To me, it looked like a Hollywood set. My mother saw it as a place to escape our neighborhood and "broaden our horizons."

The third grade at Riverdale Country School was divided into two sections of eighteen kids each. I was the only black boy in section one. There was another black boy in section two. We found each other fast. His name was Justin, and we bonded the first time we met. We had the same haircut, a towering box cut, like one of our favorite rappers, Big Daddy Kane. Daddy Kane's high-top was as chiseled as a statue. It was the gold standard.

Justin lived in the Soundview Projects, just minutes away from our house in the Bronx. My mother looked after Justin as if he were one of her own. His mom, Carol, did the same for me. Our moms were close. Carol was also a single mother working multiple jobs to send her kids to private school. She didn't speak to Justin's dad, Eddie, anymore, but Justin did. I really looked up to Eddie. I loved going with Justin to visit him in Harlem. Eddie had been a Black Panther in the 1970s. Now he worked as a bus driver and a poet. I thought he treated Justin and me like grown-ups. I always listened carefully when Eddie spoke.

"We are black males, and as black males there are certain things we have to deal with that others don't," he told us once. "Just like every kind of person has problems that only they have to cope with. As black men, we have to carry that weight and stay strong and proud."

• • •

Two years after we'd started at Riverdale, Justin and I entered the fifth grade. Standing almost five feet six, he loomed over me, and his skinny frame made him appear even taller. His voice was deep. Puberty hit him before the rest of the class. His physical maturity came with emotional maturity. He had a calm way of seeing through anyone's phony act.

One day we spent the afternoon in Manhattan, prowling sneaker stores for new Nikes we couldn't afford. On the Number 2 train home, we were crushed in a crowd of executives, construction workers, accountants, and maids. Hands of all colors clung to the metal pole in the middle of the subway car.

Justin broke down his strategy for securing a seat. "Just stand next to the white people. They'll get off by a Hundred and Tenth Street. I swear, you'll see. Give it six more stops." I grinned at him, then nodded in awe as his prediction came true. All the suits emptied the train by the time we hit 110th Street, the last wealthy stop in Manhattan. Seats on both sides cleared as though the Red Sea had parted, and we plopped down, relieving ourselves of the weight of our backpacks. The train's last yuppie scurried through the closing doors. A subway car full of blacks and Latinos would continue the ride up to Harlem and the Bronx.

Justin and I got off the graffitied train at Gun Hill Road. Everything about the Bronx was more intense than downtown Manhattan. Even the name of the street we walked down—Gun Hill Road—held the threat of blood sport. Once we hit the Bronx bricks, different food smells wafted through the air: beef patties and curried goat from the Jamaican spot, deep-fried dumplings and chicken wings from the Chinese take-out joint, cuchifritos from the Puerto Rican lunch counter. Up and down the street were people hustling everything from mix tapes to T-shirts to incense. The air rang with English and Spanish in every imaginable accent. By now, all of this was home to me.

We were headed to Ozzie's to see our crew. Ozzie had been my boy since that first basketball game. He was tall and dark-skinned, with a close-cropped caesar and a soft Caribbean accent. Everyone was already there, sprawled out on the white stone steps of his house.

My boy Paris gave me a dap. He was a tough, good-looking guy with a brilliant smile, which he rarely shared.

"You find Nikes?" Paris asked.

"Naw, too expensive," I said.

"Yeah? But you gotta keep it fresh in Riverdale, don't you? How y'all like it up there at the white school?" Paris leaned back as he spoke—his question was a challenge.

"It's cool, it's whatever," I quietly replied, looking down at the ground. It was a sore spot. In the hood, your school affiliation was all-important. You got some of your rep from your school, and the name Riverdale wasn't impressing anyone. Most of my friends attended public school in the area; a few went to Catholic school. Justin and I were the only two who actually took an hour-and-a-half trip crosstown to attend a pricey school where we were among the very few splotches of color. It made the crew suspicious of us.

I quickly changed the subject. "What's up with the Knicks this year?"

"Nah, for real, what's up with Riverdale?" Paris asked. His voice rose on the last word as he made his best attempt at a proper British accent. He wasn't going to drop this. I had to admit that the name had a 1950s white-picket-fence ring to it. It was embarrassing.

I stayed casual. "Yeah, I told you, it's cool, man, nobody messes with me over there. I've got the place on lock." From the corner of my eye, I caught Justin shaking his head with amazement at the nonsense dribbling out of my mouth. I could feel the burn of his skeptical stare on the side of my face, but I pushed on.

"Let me tell you how I run things up there," I said, and I launched into the story of my recent suspension from school. A few weeks earlier I had been suspended for fighting. I was playfully wrestling with a kid from my grade and went in for a killer move: I grabbed his right arm with mine and hoisted him over my shoulder, then dropped him hard on the ground. The fall was awkward, and he landed on his head, opening a small but surprisingly bloody cut. After the boy was rushed to the school nurse and eventually to the hospital to get a few stitches, I was suspended.

That was the truth.

For Paris and the gang, I decided to juice the story up a little. "So the other day, this joker," I began, "he was disrespecting me, so I get up in his face! I get close to him to say 'You gonna keep talking?' and he says nothing. So I pick him up over my head and slam him to the ground. I'm standing over his body—he's bleeding at this point—and I'm taunting him like Muhammad Ali over Sonny Liston! I'm like, 'I *dare* you to get back up!'"

Everyone looked to Justin as a witness. Justin was grimacing. He knew my attempt to sound legendary was, in fact, just a legend. And he let the rest of them know it, too. The more I blushed, the more they cracked up, and vice versa. I was saved from their mocking when a man stumbled toward us. His hair looked as if it hadn't seen a comb in weeks. His sneakers were caked with dirt and only one of them had a lace.

"C-c-can you young brothers spare some change? I n-n-need to make a phone call," he stuttered. An odor like that of rotten fruit surrounded him.

Ozzie responded first, his Jamaican accent a little thicker than usual. "Get out of here, man. Nobody has any change for you."

The man slowly shuffled away, looking back over his shoulder every few steps, as if he was expecting one of us to overrule Ozzie's rejection. Ozzie shook his head in disbelief and said, "If the dude wanted to buy some rock, he should have just said it. Who was he gonna call if we gave him some change?" We all laughed as the man staggered back up the block to look for sympathy elsewhere.

Drugs were not new to the Bronx. Marijuana, cocaine, and heroin had been around for ages. But crack was different. It was easy to get and insanely strong—and addictive. After it hit the scene in the early 1980s, it didn't take long for crack to put a stranglehold on many communities. The Bronx was one of them. I was an eyewitness. My friends and I traded stories we'd overheard or things we'd seen: A father left his family and robbed his parents for money to buy rock. A pregnant mother sold her body to get another hit. Someone's grandmother blew her monthly Social Security check on the drug.

Crack was also different in the way it got passed around. There was so much money to be made that drug gangs started hiring more and more people to work for them. Some of my best friends got sucked into the game. The surge in drugs was matched by a surge in guns. Guns not only became more accessible, they became more sophisticated. What my grandparents called "foolishness" spread from the gangs to the rest of the neighborhood. Turf wars got deadly fast. There was fear on all sides.

And just as bad, everyone was on the defensive. From the early 1980s to the end of the decade, there was an almost 61 percent jump in the murder rate in New York City.

When I look back now, it's almost surreal. In 2008, there were 417 homicides in the city. In 1990, there were 2,605. Those murders were concentrated in a handful of neighborhoods, and the victims were mostly from a single demographic group: young black men. You would've been safer living in a war zone than in some of those neighborhoods. We laughed at the panhandler outside Ozzie's house that day, but there were thousands of people like him throughout the city.

The sun was beginning to set, so Justin and I knew we didn't have much time to get home. We didn't need to check our watches—we were starting to feel the fear that crept around the edges at dusk.

"Stay cool, tough guy!" Paris cooed at me as Justin and I walked off. I shook my head to show I didn't take him seriously.

Taking the subway home after dark was a different journey from the one we'd made in the afternoon. There were rules to follow: Never look people in the eye. Don't smile; it makes you look weak. If someone yells for you, just keep walking. Always keep your money in your front pocket, never in your back pocket. Know where the dealers and smokers are at all times. Know where the cops are at all times. Justin and I kept a strut in our step, tried to keep it cool, but as we made our way to the train, we were practically speed walking.

"Did you study yet for the English test on Wednesday?" Justin asked.

"Nope," I said.

"You know they're going to put you on probation if you don't start doing better, man."

I knew. But I didn't like getting a lecture from him, in addition to the ones I got at home.

"The problem isn't what I study or don't study," I began. "The problem is that they don't understand my whole situation. I mean, I've got a long trip to and from school every day. Not to mention that my father is dead, my mother is overworked . . ."

I trailed off when I felt Justin's withering glare. Justin had it as hard as I did, worse in some ways, but he still got the best grades in the class. For a moment we didn't speak. I wanted to break the awkwardness.

"Know what?" I said. "My mother's starting to threaten me with military school if I don't get my grades together."

He laughed. "For real?"

I nodded. It was true. "She even got her hands on a brochure. As if she's actually looking into it!"

But I knew there was no way my mother would allow her only son to be shipped off to military school. Regardless of the grades. Regardless of the suspensions. It was too far, too permanent. Maybe she'd shift me to a school closer to home, maybe a public or Catholic school, but not a military school. And she needed a man in the house to look after Shani and Nikki, not to mention her, right? In Caribbean households, boys were treated like princes. She was bluffing. And what was military school anyway? A bunch of country folks, waving flags and chewing tobacco, screaming at kids to crawl through mud. And why—to prepare them to get killed in a war? My mother wouldn't even let me have toy guns in the house. It was absurd.

"We'll see what happens," Justin said with a smirk.

"Yeah, we'll see," I confidently replied.

I started to think about Paris. What I couldn't express to him and the other guys was that I felt weird about Riverdale, too. I got a crazy current of emotions whenever I stepped onto campus. Every time I looked around at the buildings and the trees and the view of the river, I was reminded of the sacrifices my mother was making to keep me there. And every time I looked at my fellow students, I was reminded of how little I fit in. I was trying to control the conflicting emotions of thankfulness and resentfulness, appreciation and self-consciousness.

I remembered that on the bus to school one day, Justin and I were talking about starting junior high soon. There we would have the option of taking French, Spanish, or Latin.

"Psh! Who needs another language? We're already bilingual!" Justin had laughed. It was basically true. We spoke a whole other language at Riverdale than we did at home. It was like being double agents or superheros—we had another identity off that campus. It was stressful. I felt like a chameleon. Justin did, too. If we wanted to fit in with our crew, we had to act a certain way. If we wanted to fit in with the kids at school, we had to act another way. And we wanted to fit in with both—very different—groups. But we wanted to do it on our own terms, by being "ourselves." I was having a difficult time understanding what that meant, and I also felt the burden of representing something bigger than myself. There was this increasing need to wear the mask wherever I went, and the mask seemed to change based on the audience.

It wasn't just that Justin and I were a different race from our Riverdale classmates, though. It was also about money. The Riverdale kids had it. I hid the fact that my family was drastically poorer than everyone else's. Every week I created a schedule for my clothes. I had three "good" shirts and three "good" pairs of pants. I would rotate the order in which I wore them, mixing and matching so that each day I had on a fresh combination. Later I even borrowed Nikki's clothes to show some further variation, thinking that nobody would notice the zippers at the bottoms of the jeans or the way the hips hugged a little tight. I would just nonchalantly say that I was trying to "bring the seventies back." This claim was usually met with polite smiles when I was in the room, but I can only imagine the hysterical laughter when I wasn't around.

When the kids would talk about the new video game system that was out or how their family was going to Greece or Spain or France during summer vacation, I would sit silent, hoping they wouldn't ask me where my family planned on "summering." At times I would try to join in, talking about the "vacation home" my family had in Brooklyn. The "vacation home" I was speaking about was the church where my grandfather led a congregation. But Flatbush Avenue wasn't exactly the French Riviera.

Whenever I hung out with my school friends, we went to

their homes, not mine. I was ashamed of being embarrassed about my own home, but I didn't want to have to explain our differences to them. One day, I broke my own rule. It was my uncle Howard's idea. He was my mom's brother, and he always kept an eye on me. I think he sensed my frustration with living in separate worlds and thought sports could unite my neighborhood friends and my wealthier classmates. Because of Uncle Howard, I invited ten friends from school to come and play baseball against us in the neighborhood.

In the first inning, my neighborhood friend Deshawn, who was playing first base, started trash-talking Randy. Randy was a lanky Riverdale kid with a mop of sandy brown hair. He took Deshawn's teasing pretty well, but I could see after a while it was starting to wear on him. Laughing, Randy playfully tipped the bill of Deshawn's cap, knocking it off his head. Deshawn's death stare silenced Randy's laugh. It was as if he were a king and someone had thrown his crown into the dirt. Before we were even fifteen minutes into the game, they were rolling around in the grass. Three fights and four innings later, it was clear my experiment wasn't working out. The game was called. All the players retreated to their separate corners, to their separate worlds.

All except me, still caught in the middle.

Four

KID KUPID'S LAST STRIKE

*"**Leave the smack** and the crack for the wack*
Or the vial and the nine; keep a smile like that."

My eyes were closed, and my hands drummed out the beat as if I were laying down the tracks on a DJ set. I was in the zone; even if I was only in the front seat of my mother's blue Honda Civic. I recited a verse from the Chubb Rock song as it blared out of the car's speakers.

My mother took her eyes off the road and looked at me. I could see she was shocked and angry.

I kept reciting lyrics as though I'd written them myself.

> *"Anyway the shunless one brings forth the fun*
> *No hatred; the summer's almost done."*

"Wes! How long have you known that song?"
"I dunno. Not long," I mumbled out the window. I was

eleven. Responding to my mother in complete sentences wasn't my top priority.

"Well, your grades obviously aren't bad because you can't pick stuff up or because you're stupid. You're just not working hard enough!" my mother said, her voice rising with a healthy mix of excitement and annoyance at her revelation. After a series of unsatisfactory report cards, she had started to believe that my teachers' assertions might be correct: I might have a learning disability. My teachers had broken it down for her more than once: "Wes is a nice boy, but he has real problems retaining information." But now she was having second thoughts.

"How can you recite these lyrics from a rap song but at the same time be struggling with English class?"

I didn't respond. My silence made her fuming mad; I could feel her anger in the air.

What she didn't know was that my problem with school was much more basic than goofing off or having a learning disability. The real problem was that I wasn't even showing up half the time.

Some days I would check into school for attendance. Other days, after I put on my backpack and waved goodbye to my grandparents, I'd stick around the neighborhood and meet up with one of the guys who had a similar arrangement. My sister Shani was a loyal accomplice; she never snitched.

It took a couple of weeks to get my schedule down pat. I realized the only time anyone really cared about my attendance was during homeroom. Two days of the week, I had homeroom with my English teacher, Mrs. Downs. She'd noticed that I was just showing up when I felt like it, and when I did show up, I'd spend the whole class perfecting my role as class clown. She thought of me as the bad apple in the class. One day, she flatly told me that it didn't matter to her if I showed up because the class ran more smoothly when I wasn't there. From that moment, I understood that Mrs. Downs and I had an unspoken agreement, a "don't ask, don't tell" pact that worked for both of us. She didn't want me there disrupting, and I didn't want to be there.

I liked being popular and I liked my friends, but I was sick of being divided between Riverdale and the hood. I was too "rich" for the kids from the neighborhood and too "poor" for the kids at school. I was forgetting how to act naturally, and I was tangled in the contradictions between my two worlds. It took too much effort to seem effortless. My confidence was taking a hard hit, and my grades were slipping with it. Ds were a disappointment, but Cs were satisfactory, and Bs were cause for celebration.

"You don't start putting some of that energy into your grades, there's going to be trouble, Wes. You think I'm playing. Just try me," Mom snapped, and then she returned her full attention to the road, as if to say "case closed." I was glad she stopped talking then, because the new EPMD song came on. She must have noticed my slight nod to the beat, because she quickly killed the radio and put Whitney Houston's "The Greatest Love of All" in the tape deck.

"*Again?*" I groaned.

My mother pretended not to hear me. She had been playing this song on repeat for months now. She wanted the uplifting lyrics to sink in and inspire me. I thought they were corny.

Hip-hop had begun to play a special role in my life. It wasn't just music and lyrics. In my struggle to reconcile my two worlds, it was like a guardian angel. By the late 1980s, hip-hop had grown from being an underground art in the Bronx to a rising global culture. My obsession with hip-hop kept me credible with the kids in my neighborhood. It let them know that, regardless of my preppy school, I still was one of them. Hip-hop also gave the kids in my school a point of entry into my life: Public Enemy's black nationalist anthems or KRS-One's pulpy fantasies about gunning down crack dealers offered a window into my world. Before hip-hop, my home turf had seemed foreign to those who bothered to think about it at all.

But even more than that, I found in hip-hop the sound of my generation talking to itself, working through the fears and anxieties and dreams—of wealth or power or revolution or success—we all shared. Music was a way to broadcast what was going on in *our* world to the rest of the world. It made us feel less alone in the madness of the era, less pushed to the margins.

Of course, my love for hip-hop didn't matter to my mother. She was sick of my bad report cards when she was working so hard to send me to a good school. She caught on that being a class clown was part of my school personality, and she didn't like it. "No one's hiring you to be Eddie Murphy in that classroom, Wes. He's paid to be funny, you just get in trouble," she would say, hand on her hip. She wanted me to get serious, and soon.

I didn't act out at home. I was sneaking away from school, but I tried to keep up with family duties. I felt that as long as I wasn't causing trouble in my home, I could avoid serious punishment. Our mother worked so much, and our grandparents were older and tired; I knew they needed my help and that my sisters and I were supposed to look after one another. But Nikki had all she could handle with her own turbulent high school experience, which was about to come to a close. The move to the Bronx had been hard on her. She attended three different high schools in four years and never fully adjusted to any of them. Shani was different; she was a star in the classroom. She didn't go outside much, except to play basketball with me and my friends, and she seemed to have a book with her wherever she went. In fact, by the time I hit fifth grade and she was in third grade, she had overtaken me in reading scores, a distinction she maintained through our entire academic lives.

One day I found her in the living room, a bloodstained napkin stuck in one of her nostrils and my grandmother's arms wrapped around her shoulders. Shani had been jumping rope with her friend Lateshia and a Puerto Rican girl named Ingrid. A fight broke out, words were exchanged, and Shani got a punch to the nose. Shani was much bigger than Lateshia and was used to wrestling with me, but she didn't fight back. She'd started crying and headed into the house, pinching her nose to stop the bleeding.

By the end of the story, I was furious. First at Shani for not fighting back, but above all at Lateshia, who'd had the audacity to go after my sister. I had recently seen *The Godfather* for the first time, so I pulled a mob move and flew out the door to find Lateshia.

No one messes with my family, I thought, channeling Sonny Corleone. My actual godmother, who was standing by the door, also wanted in on the action. Aunt BB, a tall, light-skinned Alabamian who had known my grandparents since she'd moved up to New York thirty years earlier, was one of our family's fiercest defenders, and she wanted to play her part in avenging Shani. She followed me up the street. In retrospect, we made a comical pair of warriors—a forty-something-year-old woman marching after an eleven-year-old boy, ready for a showdown with a little girl. But we were stone cold serious.

Lateshia was sitting on the front steps with her older brother. She straightened with a surprised look when she saw us roll up. Aunt BB demanded to know why she'd hit Shani. Lateshia stumbled through an answer, claiming that she'd been defending herself.

Aunt BB cut her off. "Little girl, don't you ever touch her again. I don't know who you think you are, but you are really messing with the wrong one."

Lateshia stared back. She was too cool to show submission and too scared to show defiance. I faced Lateshia while keeping an eye on her older brother.

"And let me tell you," I said, "if I ever hear about you touching her again, the last thing you will have to worry about is a bloody nose." Not only was her brother older and bigger than me, he also had a rep as one not to be played with. But I just stood there in my b-boy stance, empowered by strains of "The Bridge Is Over" running through my head, until I felt like the message had gotten across.

Satisfied, Aunt BB and I took off for our house. I was a little shaken as we walked back home in the twilight. Little things like this had a way of escalating into blood feuds. Big brothers called bigger brothers, who called crews for backup. But Shani never played with Lateshia again and, fortunately, I never saw her brother again.

The Bronx street had become a fixture in my life. Whether I was playing ball at Gun Hill Projects basketball court, heading over to Three Boys on Burke Avenue to get a slice of pizza, or just sprawling out on stoops with my crew, I learned some of the most important lessons in my life on these streets. I learned about girls getting periods not from biology class but from my friend Paris. I learned the realities of gang violence not from after-school specials but from when my boy Mark got jumped and beaten down for wearing the wrong color jacket. And I learned that cops on the corner of Laconia Avenue were smarter than I thought.

It was a warm Saturday in October and I was leaving the basketball courts after a game when out of the corner of my eye I saw Shea, one of my friends from the neighborhood. Shea was my age, but he was shorter, with reddish hair and light skin, light enough for a spray of freckles to shine through. I broke off from my friends to ask him what he was up to. "Nothing," he said confidently, "just finished working."

I checked out his gear: black jeans, a white tank top, and a black backpack. Work. I knew exactly what that meant. Shea was a "runner"—a rookie position in any drug enterprise. A runner was the one who moved packages from drug suppliers to the dealers. The suppliers used kids like Shea because they were less likely to be stopped by police officers. Shea was making decent money, and ever since he'd started "working," my friends and I had seen less of him.

Shea and I sat in front of the Cue Lounge, a bar and billiards club in between a Kentucky Fried Chicken and a motel. Cars whizzed by. We were checking out the black wall of the lounge: it was littered with spray-painted tags. We recognized some as our friends' and others from other walls around the neighborhood. It seemed as if everybody in the hood had a nickname and a tag. Mine was simple: a "KK" with a circle around it, standing for "Kid Kupid," an alter ego I'd made up to sound as if I were popular with girls.

As we admired the wall, Shea pulled his backpack in front of him and slowly unzipped it. I peeked inside. Beside a small bottle of water and a white headband were two spray paint bottles, one with a white top and one with a blue. He looked at me with a sly smirk. "You wanna tag?"

Shea was one of the most respected young hustlers in the neighborhood. Some kids were disgusted by what he did; others respected his power and cash and kept begging him to get on. At this point, I fell somewhere in between. I couldn't say no. Plus, I loved throwing my name up on a wall. It felt like splashing in the shallow end of the criminal pool.

I scanned the streets for cops and nosy neighbors as I reached into his bag and pulled out the can with the white top. I shook the can, making sure the contents were mixed so that the paint would come out even and clean. Once I felt the coast was clear, I began to draw, starting with the connected Ks and finishing with a wide circle around them, in my custom style. Seven seconds and done. I had added my mark to Laconia Avenue, a testament to the world that Wes Moore lived—or at least Kid Kupid did. Nobody could ever deny I was there.

Wuap, wuap! The distinctive sound of the police siren rang out. Shea and I whirled around to look at each other, eyes big, and then sprinted off in different directions. I tried to run past the police car. It only took a couple of seconds for one of the cops to wrap me in his grip and throw me against his vehicle. Shea had a shot. I saw him sprinting in the opposite direction. He turned around, saw me being patted down, and tried to speed up. Seconds later, he was getting wrapped up by the other policeman. As I lay on the hood of the car with the officer's hands pressing against every part of me, searching me, I watched Shea twenty feet away on the ground getting the same treatment. I didn't know what to expect next.

The officer reached above my head and began to pull my left arm behind my back. Now I understood where this was going. I was being arrested.

"Chill, man, I didn't do anything!" I began screaming as I tried to wrangle my hands free.

"Stop resisting," the officer warned as he cuffed my left wrist and roughly pinned down my flailing right arm.

From my position on the hood of the police car, I could see an older woman staring at me, shaking her head. After cuffing me, the cop opened the back door of his cruiser, pushed my head down, and shoved me into the backseat. I was terrified. My mother was going to have to pick me up from jail. She had just finished talking to me about my grades, and now this. Our relationship had been in a strange place lately. We weren't getting along. I pretended to be independent, but really I wanted nothing more than to make her proud. I was scared of disappointing her, but too prideful to act like it mattered.

I didn't want to be like Shea, an aspiring drug dealer, but here I was, arrested alongside him. Right now, real friendship seemed far away. The kids in my crew loved one another, but how long would we mourn if any one of us disappeared? I'd seen it happen already, kids leaving the hood in one way or another—killed, imprisoned, shipped off to distant relatives down south. The older kids would pour out a little liquor or leave a shrine on a corner under a graffiti mural, or they'd reminisce about the ones who were locked up. But then life went on. The struggle went on. Who really cared? Besides my mother, who would *truly* miss me if I went to jail?

My eyes watered as I sat in the backseat, watching out the window as the two cops led Shea toward the car. Shea winked at me as he walked with his hands behind his back. Is this dude serious? I thought.

The car door opened, and Shea was thrown into my lap. "Psh! Friggin' jakes, man," he mumbled coolly as he straightened himself up.

"Yo, shut up, man! We are in serious trouble! I can't go to jail, man!" I was almost hyperventilating.

"Just say you didn't do anything. Say you don't know what they're talking about," Shea said.

I looked out the window at the two cops searching Shea's bag, and I realized that Shea's strategy was one of the dumbest ideas I had heard in a long time. Even I, who could come up with an excuse for anything, was at a loss for a good one in this situation.

The cops stood outside for what seemed like forever, discussing our fate. I wanted to ask Shea if he had any of his "work" in the bag, too, but decided against it, feeling it was better for me not to know. In fact, I didn't even want to talk to him. I wanted to wait in silence.

One of the officers, a stocky Italian with jet-black hair, moved toward the front passenger-side door and opened it. He folded himself into the car and looked back at us over his left shoulder. Shea stared back with cocky, smug indifference.

"Just what were you thinking?" the cop asked.

Almost simultaneously, Shea launched into his "It wasn't us!" story while I talked over him loudly with "I'm *really* sorry, I *swear* it won't happen again!" When we were done with our overlapping monologues, we glared at each other.

The cop shook his head and pointed his index finger at us. "You kids are way too young to be in this situation. But you know what, I see kids like you here every day. If you don't get smart, I guarantee I'll be seeing you again. That's the sad part."

He looked into our eyes, searching for a reaction. I was on the verge of tears. I was wincing because the handcuffs hurt my wrists, but I was also scared of what was going to happen next. And the self-righteous look on Shea's face made me mad. In my outlaw fantasies I would've been as defiant as Shea, but now rebellion seemed less glamorous and its consequences all too real. The moment the officer had tightened the second handcuff was when the realization struck me. Right then, I became aware that this man now had control of my body. I couldn't even use my own hands.

More than that, though, it seemed like he had control of my destiny. The possibility of going to prison opened up in front of me like a black hole. All I wanted to do was turn around, go home, and never find myself in this situation again. Kid Kupid! What was I thinking?

The cops got out of the car and opened the two back doors. The officer who'd been lecturing us gripped my shoulder and pulled me out. I heard a jingle of keys. The cuff on my left wrist opened up.

"I hope you really listened to what I told you," he said seriously, opening up the other cuff to free both of my hands.

"Yeah, thank you," I replied as I rubbed each wrist with the opposite hand.

"All right, guys, the bag is ours. Now get moving."

Shea, who had also been pulled out of the car, looked as though he was about to start protesting to them about keeping the bag until I grabbed him by the arm, telling him to get moving. We began to walk back down Allerton Avenue, turning around every few seconds to check on the cops, who were still staring at us. The police gave us a gift that day, and I swore I would never get caught in a situation like that again.

However, the next week Kid Kupid was on the loose again, more emboldened than ever.

● ● ●

My mother hadn't found out about my run-in with the cops. But she had other reasons to argue with me.

The final straw came one evening when she got a call from the dean at Riverdale, explaining why I was on academic and disciplinary probation. Bad grades, absence from classes, and an incident with a smoke bomb were just some of the reasons he rattled off. My mother sat silently on the couch with the phone to her ear.

Meanwhile, upstairs, Shani and I sat in my room trying to watch TV. Our eighteen-inch color television, topped with a wire hanger where the antenna should have been, was a blizzard of static. I got bored and looked around for alternative entertainment. I began to lightly punch Shani's arm, first with my right fist, then with my left, trying to get her to pay attention to me. She stubbornly stared ahead.

"Stop," she said, never taking her eyes off the screen.

I kept on aiming blows at her shoulder. I was feeling the kind of boredom that makes you want to create chaos. Finally fed up, Shani turned to me. "Sto—" she started to say, and as she did, the knuckles of my right hand skipped off her shoulder and into her bottom lip. Her lip was immediately stained red.

In more shock than pain, Shani saw this as an opportunity. "Oooooh, I'ma get you now," she teased. She smiled slyly as the blood covered her bottom row of teeth. Like magic, her smile faded and her bottom lip began to tremble. Her eyes filled with tears. Then came the scream.

"*Mommy!* Westley hit me in the face and I'm bleeding really bad!"

Busted.

"Shani, don't go to Mom, c'mon," I pleaded. She pushed past me to the door and sprinted down the hallway. Her acting was stellar. I knew the evidence was against me. There was nothing left to do but wait. I stared at the snowy TV screen.

When I heard my mother coming up the stairs, I braced myself. She'd be tired from her long day at work and disappointed from the conversation she'd just had with my dean. Now she'd be furious for sure. I was dreading the arguing that was about to happen when she entered the room. But it turned out she had nothing to say. She simply pulled her right hand back and slapped me.

The entire left side of my face burned. I was shocked, but I refused to show fear or weakness. I stood there looking at her. She was expecting tears or apologies. When neither came, she unloaded another slap to my face and waited for a reaction. My jaws clenched, and my hands balled into fists. By this time, I was five inches taller than she was, and my recently defined shoulders, biceps, and triceps made me look older than my age. Every reflex inside said to strike back, but I didn't. How could I? Even when we fought, she was my everything. The person I loved and respected most in my world. I had no idea what to do.

Neither did my mother, it seemed. Her almond-shaped eyes were overflowing with anger, disappointment, and confusion, and maybe even a little fear. I would never have hit my mother. But in my room, at that moment, she wasn't so sure. She looked at me as if for the first time. The days when she could physically intimidate me were clearly over. She turned around and walked out of the room. Her silence devastated me. We didn't know it at the time, but once we were each alone, we both started to cry.

Five
PLEBE

"Get up! Get up and get out of your racks, plebes!"

It was five-thirty in the morning, my room was pitch-dark, and the sound of half a dozen teenagers screaming at the tops of their lungs startled me awake. I was on the top bunk of a metal bed. My roommate, Jason, was awake, too—I could tell because he jumped out of the bottom bunk and stared up at me; even in the dark I could see the panic on his face.

"Moore, we have to get up and go in the hallway!" he said. His pubescent voice was cracking from the stress. As he waited for me to respond, he shuffled his feet as if he had to go to the bathroom. I watched him do his pee-pee dance for a moment, then peeked over at our clock, which sat across the room. I couldn't believe it.

"Bro, it is five-thirty in the morning! Tell them to come get me around eight," I said, and I yanked my covers tighter around me. "I should be ready to go then."

Dumbfounded, Jason opened his mouth to say something. Another yell came from the corridor, a single voice now, ordering us into the hallway. Jason shifted his attention; he wasn't going to waste his time trying to convince me to get up. I was either really brave or really stupid, and he wasn't going to wait around to see which.

Soon I was alone in the room.

I rolled over, turning my back to the door, and pulled the covers over my head to avoid the commotion coming from the hallway. Seconds after getting comfortable, I heard the yelling voice with a new clarity. It was on the other side of my door.

"Why is there only one person outside this room?"

My door whacked open, and in walked First Sergeant Anderson, a high school senior with the personality of a bulldog. Still half asleep, I heard the sound of boots approaching my bunk. And then they stopped. That was when the screaming started.

"Get your goat-smelling tail out of the rack! I am going to smoke you so bad, they will need dental records to identify your body! You better get that z-monster off your back, turdbird!"

I didn't know the meaning of some of these curses, but I could figure out they weren't compliments.

Why in the world was he yelling so early in the morning? And who did he think he was, screaming at me like that?

I slowly sat up and wiped my eyes. The first sergeant paused for a moment—he saw me moving and must've figured his tantrum had done the trick. I removed my hand from my eyes and calmly spoke: "Man, if you don't get out of my room . . ."

His eyes widened, then narrowed to little slits. His angry face broke into a devilish smile. Just as quickly as he'd come into the room, he disappeared.

I smirked to think that I could make one of them leave my room so easily. I was from the Bronx, after all; these country jokers must've been seriously intimidated.

Moments later the door burst open again. My entire chain of command, eight large teenagers, entered the room. Without saying a word, they picked my mattress up off the top bunk and turned it over. I dropped five feet to the cold, hard, green-tiled floor.

Welcome to the first day of military school.

I had known my mother was considering sending me away, but I never thought she'd actually do it. Valley Forge Military Academy is in Wayne, Pennsylvania, just twenty-five minutes outside Philadelphia. It's on a rolling campus surrounded by trees. It looked to me like a stricter, more formal version of Riverdale Country School, and it was an even farther cry from my Bronx neighborhood.

Every day at Valley Forge began before the sun came up and ended well after it set. Over our first few days we learned how to shine our shoes using Kiwi black shoe polish, a cotton rag, and a pretty gross amount of saliva. We learned how to execute military commands and repeat our drills so many times that "right face," "left face," and "parade rest" became as familiar as our own names. We learned how to "square the corridors," which required marching around the entire hallway to leave the building, even if the exit was only a few steps away from your room. Our birth names were irrelevant. Our past lives and our past accomplishments and failures didn't matter. We were the same now. We were nothing. In fact, we were less than nothing. We were plebes.

Plebe system is a process all new arrivals must go through in order to earn the title of "new cadet." As a plebe, you refer to yourself in the third person: "This plebe would like to go to the bathroom." "This plebe requests permission to eat." In plebe system, your plebe brothers are all you have to make it through. There is no communication with the outside world. There are no phone calls, no televisions, no radios, no visits. When you're a plebe you're like a freshman— you're the rookie on campus.

My squad leader was Sergeant Austin, a blond sophomore from Connecticut with green eyes and a sneaky smile. He would go off on one of us and then announce, "Don't take this personally, I hate you all just the same." I was given this "reassurance" more than most.

For those first few days, I was furious. The target of my rage was my mother. How could she send me away? How could she force me into a military school before I was even a teenager? When she dropped me off the first day, I had my "screw the world" face on, ready for battle—but inside I was bewildered. I felt betrayed. And I felt more alone than ever.

By the end of the fourth day at military school, I had run away four times. I had heard that there was a station somewhere in Wayne where I could catch a train that would eventually get me to Penn Station in New York, which would take me to the Number 2 subway train, which would drop me off on those grimy streets that would take me home. I had the entire plan set. The only thing I couldn't figure out was how to get to this train station in Wayne.

One morning, Jason and I were in our room shining our shoes. He was from Brooklyn; we were the only two New Yorkers in the entire unit. I considered him partly to blame for my being in military school, too: it was his grandmother who'd told my mother about Valley Forge in the first place. Jason's uncle had graduated from the school and was now a successful business executive. My mom was impressed. There was no military history in my family, but for her, as for many in immigrant families, the thought of raising a child to be an American hero was a cherished dream. Burning with resentment, I glanced at Jason.

I had just finished shining the tip of my left shoe and was scooping out a helping of polish for the right shoe when our door opened.

"Ten-hut!" my roommate yelled, jumping to his feet upon seeing our squad leader enter the room. I followed suit. Sergeant Austin looked directly at Jason and told him to leave the room. Jason quickly scurried out. I was afraid something bad was about to happen, and that Austin had cleared out because he didn't want anyone to witness it. I braced myself. I didn't know what I'd done this time, but it couldn't be good.

"Sit down," Austin said.

I dropped into my chair but stayed tense. Austin sat across from me like we were old buddies about to have a heart-to-heart.

"Listen, Moore," he said, "you don't want to be here, and, quite honestly, we don't want you here. So I drew you a map of how to get to the train station." Then he handed me a worn notebook. At the back of the book was a map with handwritten directions to the train station.

I looked at the map, stunned. All I wanted was to leave this place. To see my mother. Here was my squad leader, for whom I had no love, giving me what felt like one of the greatest gifts I had ever received. The weight of loneliness was suddenly lifted. This map was my path to freedom.

Happiness overwhelmed me. I couldn't help smiling broadly, and thanked him. "I will never forget you!" I proclaimed.

He rolled his eyes. "Yeah, just get out of here." He stood up from the chair. I got up and snapped to attention, showing the first real sign of respect for him since I'd walked through the gates. As he shut the door behind him, my mind was spinning.

I began to plan my great escape.

At ten every night, we had to listen to taps play in the main parade area before lights-out. Taps is a hauntingly slow bugle call played to signal the end of the day. It's also played at military funerals. At Valley Forge Military Academy, the entire corps would stop and stand in the parade rest position until the final note died away. That night I bowed my head but couldn't suppress a smile. I knew this would be the last time I would have to endure this depressing melody.

I set my alarm for midnight. That would be late enough for everyone to be asleep but early enough to give me a head start before wake-up call. My alarm clock sat under my pillow so only I would hear it. My overnight bag was packed. I had a flashlight, a few changes of clothes, and a granola bar. I was ready to go.

Two hours after taps, I was tiptoeing through the hallways until I hit the bloodred door that took me into the night. With nothing but the bag slung over my shoulder, I clutched the map in one hand, the flashlight in the other. I quietly bolted through the door without looking back.

Goodbye and good riddance! I thought.

The night was pitch-black. I followed the map. It led me through bushes and brush that quickly turned into trees and woods. I figured in a couple of steps the trees would open up and reveal the train station sitting there waiting for me. Minutes later, that hope was fading. In its place was a different feeling: terror.

This feels like the beginning of a bad horror movie, I thought as I trolled through the forest. I imagined hearing snakes and bears and other wild animals. I was losing my cool. Finally I sat down on a rock that I could have sworn I had just tripped over ten paces back. I began to cry. I was defeated. I had never wanted anything more in my life than to leave that school, and I was realizing that it was not going to happen.

As I sat on the rock weeping, I heard the rustling of leaves and brush behind me. These sounds were *not* my imagination. I pricked up my ears, and my head snapped to attention. I turned toward the sounds and suddenly heard a chorus of laughter. Out of the darkness came the members of my chain of command, including my new "friend," Sergeant Austin.

"Son of a . . ." I trailed off, in shock. The directions he had given me were fake. They'd led me nowhere but to the middle of the woods.

Without a fight, I got up and followed them back to campus. With my head bowed, I entered the main building with them and they led me straight to my tactical officer's office.

Colonel Battaglioli, or Colonel Batt, as we called him, sat in his office as my chain of command led me in. I was broken, dead-eyed, with my overnight bag still on my shoulder and the useless map folded in my pocket. Colonel Batt was a retired U.S. Army officer with twenty-six years in the service. He had served all over the world, including combat tours in Vietnam. When he saluted, it seemed that the force of his entire body went into it. He spoke like an understudy for Al Pacino, all spit and curved vowels. He was new to the job at Valley Forge. We were his first plebe class, and I was his first major challenge.

I stood before Colonel Batt, my eyes cast down in embarrassment. "Look at me, Moore," he firmly commanded. I raised my eyes. Colonel Batt continued: "I am going to let you talk on the phone for five minutes, and that is it for the *rest* of plebe system. Call your parents, call whoever you need to, but you had better be snapped out of this when that phone hangs up."

I looked around the room and saw four members of my chain of command looking down on me. I also noticed a man I had not seen before but whose presence dominated the room, demanding not only attention but also respect. He was black, and he stood about five ten and carried a muscular 220 pounds or so. He peered down at me through his glasses with a laserlike focus. His uniform was pressed so sharp you could have cut paper with the cuffs on his khaki shorts. He appeared to be still a teenager but he had an old soul and a frighteningly serious demeanor. He didn't say a word.

Colonel Batt handed me the phone, and I dialed the only number I knew by heart. As the phone rang, I began to think about what I could say in five minutes to convince my mother to let me back home.

"Hello?" Her voice was groggy. After all, it was one in the morning.

"Hey, Ma, it's me!" I said, a little too loudly. I was excited to hear her voice after what had been the four longest days of my life.

She got nervous at the sound of my voice. "Wes! What is going on? I thought I wasn't supposed to hear from you for at least another month. Are you all right?"

"I'm fine, I'm fine. Look, I only have five minutes.

Ma, I know I haven't been perfect, but I promise to do better. I'll pay attention in school and go more often! I'll go every day!"

"Wes—"

"I'll clean my room, I'll clean *your* room, I'll—"

She cut me off. "Wes, you are not going anywhere until you give this place a try. Listen to me for a second. I am so proud of you for giving this a shot, and your father is proud of you, too. I know he is. We just want you to make an effort. Too many people have sacrificed in order for you to be there to have you leave now."

I had no idea then, but I later found out just what sacrifices she was talking about. Military school is not free. It's not even cheap. My mother had written to family and friends, asking them to help her however they could. Weeks later, she was still thousands of dollars short.

My grandparents knew that as an almost-teenager, I was at a turning point in my life.

These forks in the road can happen so fast for young boys. Within months or even weeks, our journeys can twist and turn. Sometimes there's no turning back. With no intervention—or the wrong intervention—we can be lost forever. My mother chose to intervene, and she decided that overdoing it was better than doing nothing at all. She felt that if I was going to head in the right direction, my environment needed to change. My options needed to expand. Drastically. My grandparents agreed. Now that my grandparents knew they were needed in the Bronx, the desire they'd had to move back to Jamaica had faded. Their children and grandchildren were here. Their friends and doctors were here. And more than that, they now considered themselves not Jamaicans who were living in America, but *Americans* of Jamaican descent. So they took the money they had in the home in the Bronx, decades of savings and mortgage payments, and gave it to my mother so she could pay for my first year at Valley Forge.

But that night, as I sat at the other end of the line, listening to my mother talk about sacrifice, I didn't know what my grandparents had given up.

"Running away doesn't solve anything," she continued. "It just pushes back the problem so you have to deal with it later. It doesn't make it disappear. And when you finally come around to it, it's gotten bigger and worse. Look, I love you, and I want you to do your best. And, Wes, it's time to stop running."

Then it was time to hang up. The five minutes had gone by too fast. It hurt to swallow. I knew my mother was right about pushing problems back. I had been so behind on work and studying that it had felt too late to bother starting. I'd figured it was a hopeless cause. So I'd kept not working. And my grades just got worse. And now here I was.

I was sent back to my room to lie down for the three hours before I would wake up to the same trash-can-drumming, light-flashing, music-blaring, insult-yelling wake-up call I'd gotten the day before.

The next day, as we prepared to head to second mess,

which was what they called lunch, I noticed the black man from the night before talking to Colonel Batt. They were looking in my direction for a while. Finally the two men saluted, and the black man walked back toward F Company, the college freshmen and sophomores. It was known around the entire corps as the most impressive company. Its members were the best marchers, the most athletic, the most disciplined. I wondered who this guy was. As my eyes followed him, I heard the thunderous sound of 120 men all snapping to attention. Nineteen-year-old Cadet Captain Ty Hill took his place at the front of F Company.

I knew my mom had met Cadet Captain Hill once when she was still on the fence about sending me to military school. The school had used him as an example of why I should go. He was one of the stars of Valley Forge—a college sophomore from Texas who was about to become an officer in the army.

I had never seen a young man demand that much respect from his peers. I had seen Shea get respect in the neighborhood, but this was different. This was the kind of respect you can't beat or scare out of people. In spite of myself, I was impressed.

That was when I began to understand that I was in a different environment. Not simply because I was in the middle of Pennsylvania instead of the Bronx or Baltimore. It was a different head space. Here, leadership was honored. Doing well in class didn't make you a geek, it made you a star. At Riverdale I'd felt like a leader because I was popular.

When the lesson got boring, I was the entertainment, so the other students wanted me in their classes. But here class clowns weren't dazzling anyone. If I wanted to make it through this place, I was going to have to find another way to make an impression.

My grandparents right after they moved to the united States. They were married for fifty-seven years.

Mom and Dad at their wedding. My grandmother made my mother's dress.

My dad at work. His passions in life were
his family and good journalism.

My sister,
Nikki, posing
with me.
I was two
years old.

My first month at
Valley Forge. Here, I'm
th school superintendent
Admiral Thurman.

Here I am with
my best
friend, Justin.

I felt honored that more than a dozen
members of my family came to Pennsylvania for
my high school graduation.

The "other" Wes being held by his older brother, Tony.

Tony at fourteen years old.

Wes at home in Cherry Hill.

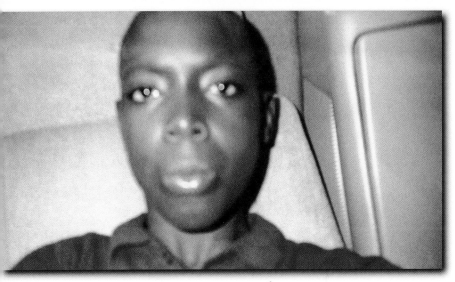

Wes in 1990, shortly after he was charged with attempted murder.

Tony had gained a fierce reputation in Baltimore by age sixteen.

Wes with his daughter when she visited him in prison.

During my last year at Valley Forge, I was the highest-ranking cadet on campus, with more than eight hundred cadets under my command.

Here I am with Nikki and Shani after a Johns Hopkins football game.

Preparing to go on a mission with Lieutenant Anthony Delsignore, a good Marine and friend.

My bride, Dawn, and me on one of the most amazing days of my life, our wedding day.

Meeting with middle-school kids in Baltimore.

Standing under the NASDAQ screen in the heart of Times Square. I rang the closing bell at the New York Stock Exchange with members of the Iraq and Afghanistan Veterans of America.

Six

REFUGE

Ding, ding.

Two bells rang through the mess hall, signaling afternoon classes. The corps moved en masse toward the cafeteria doors.

I stood up from my chair and ordered my platoon to "stand fast," or stand still, as I reminded them about the room inspection that was going to take place immediately after school.

"Yes, Sergeant," they responded, alert. They joined the flood headed toward the door.

Three years earlier I'd been one of the lowly plebes entering the gates of Valley Forge for the first time. Now I was in charge of some of them. I was a platoon sergeant, a cadet master sergeant, and, at the age of fifteen, the youngest senior noncommissioned officer in the entire corps.

The financial strain Valley Forge put on my mother had

eased after the first year, when the school gave me academic and athletic scholarships. My mother was proud. She saw how I'd changed since starting military school. My back was straight, and my sentences ended with "sir" or "ma'am." One time when I was home for summer break, she walked in on me shining my shoes and was so surprised she started laughing.

The school's motto, "No excuses, no exceptions," and our honor code, "A cadet will not lie, cheat, or steal, or tolerate those that do," were not just sentences we had to memorize. They were words to live by. With the support of my chain of command and the school faculty, I'd actually started to enjoy military school. These people made it clear that they cared about whether I succeeded. Eventually, their caring made me care, too. Having people around me who believed that I could succeed made me want to succeed.

I stopped in the mail room. I had got a letter from Justin. We exchanged dozens of letters after I left the Bronx for Pennsylvania. My leaving wasn't easy on either of us. We'd always been best friends. Once, our teacher at Riverdale pulled Justin to the side and given him a stern warning: "Justin, you're a good kid; you need to stay away from Wes or you'll end up going nowhere, just like he will." Justin ignored him.

This latest letter opened with some funny stories about school and my old hood, but a couple of paragraphs later, the tone became serious. Two pieces of news took the wind out of me. First, Shea had been arrested on drug charges. These weren't simply running or possession charges, either.

"Possession with the intent to distribute" was a charge of a completely different magnitude—with serious sentences. Justin hadn't seen Shea around the neighborhood in a while and, from the sound of it, was not sure when he would again.

The second piece of news was that Carol, Justin's mother, was dying. Over the past few years, she'd been moving more slowly and seemed just a beat off. They'd found out that she had Hodgkin's disease, a form of cancer. The survival rate is around 90 percent for those who discover it early. With his older sister away in college, and his dad, Eddie, still down in Harlem, Justin's role in the family was changing.

"Every morning I'm at the hospital with Mom," he wrote, "and then I'm off to class, late, of course. After basketball practice, I'm back at the hospital till visitors get kicked out. I'm trying to stay on top of everything, but it's too much sometimes. I don't know if I have time to be on the team anymore. My grades are way down low. . . . Wes, I'm wiped."

My heart felt crushed under the weight of his words. Even though I'd grown to enjoy military school, I still had mixed feelings, and they were eating at me. I felt guilty being away from everyone. If I were home, I could talk to Justin after he left the hospital. I didn't know what I'd say, but at least I'd be there.

I wanted to be there for my mother and my sisters, too. They were moving back to Maryland, where Shani would begin high school. I remembered how tough Baltimore could be, and I wanted to be able to help out.

I felt like being at military school was keeping me in a

bubble, ignorant of the struggles on the outside. Wearing this uniform had definitely made me feel more clearheaded than I had been a few years before, but I wondered if it was just an illusion. Once I left the campus, the world outside would still be just as crazy. Would I go back to my old ways of thinking?

● ● ●

H Company was broken up into two platoons. I was the platoon sergeant for one of them, and a cadet named Dalio was the platoon sergeant for the other. In the army, there is an old saying that the officers make the orders but the sergeants do all the work. This year, as a cadet platoon sergeant, I was learning how true that was. From the moment I woke up till the moment I went to bed, my day was spent thinking about my platoon—making sure my guys were doing well in class, making sure things were fine at home, making sure the building was clean, and on and on. I loved the responsibilities, but taking care of all of them was exhausting. Saturday evening, after taps, Dalio and I put our guys down to sleep but still had a few hours free before we had to be back on campus.

"Want to grab a stromboli?" Dalio asked. A stromboli is essentially a pizza folded over on itself—a bread, cheese, sauce, and meat concoction that was my favorite local comfort food. It was a good break from mess hall food. I was in. We threw on our dress gray uniforms with the navy ties and headed out.

We strolled down the barely lit streets into downtown Wayne, gossiping about our platoons. About ten minutes into the walk, a red Toyota with tinted windows slowly drove up to us. We figured the driver needed help navigating the dark, signless streets. We stopped and peered in.

The window rolled halfway down, releasing loud rock music and the smell of alcohol into the night air. Behind the wheel was an overweight teenager with messy black hair and a scar across the top of his forehead. "What are you guys doing?" he demanded.

"Nothing," I replied. Who is this guy? I wondered.

"Don't you mean 'Nothing, *sir*'?" a voice rang out from the backseat. Because of the tinted windows, we couldn't see who'd said it.

"Nothing, sir," I corrected myself automatically, without even knowing who made the order. I was so accustomed to the rules on campus that it took me a second to realize I might be calling some random drunk kid from town "sir."

"I am Colonel Bose's son, and not only are you rude, but your uniforms are a mess. I am going to report you both," the kid in the backseat said in a gruff voice.

Dalio and I looked at each other, confused. What kind of prank was this?

Dalio leaned down to the window. "Well, you have our names, so do what you have to do," he said.

The car sped away, leaving a trail of blaring music behind it. We continued walking down the middle of the street.

"What do you think?" Dalio asked me.

"Probably nothing. Bunch of idiots."

Then a speeding car came roaring up behind us. It was the same red Toyota, and it came within feet of running us both over. We turned around with just enough time to jump out of the way. The car slowed to a creep after missing us, like a predator waiting for its prey. It was only a few yards away from us. Dalio and I got up from the side of the road, looked at each other, and broke into a sprint. Then the car sped away.

Dalio looked at me and said, "What are we supposed to do?"

That was when the kid from the Bronx started to elbow the cadet sergeant aside. "We keep going to get our pizza," I told him. "They're done for the night. And if they aren't, we'll see them when they have the guts to get out of the car."

Dalio looked unconvinced, but he was still hungry. We picked up our pace as we walked in the shadows of the tree-lined sidewalks, now avoiding the center of the road. I felt like I was doing my speed walk to the subway in the Bronx again. There was nobody to be seen on the dark, open road. Every few minutes a car passed and made my heart stop. This was military school, I thought. We were supposed to be protected from this kind of stuff.

After a few minutes we were calmer, and our focus was back on getting that cheesy stromboli. We were crossing the intersection when I heard a voice yelling.

"Go home, nigger!"

As I whirled my head to see where the yell had come

from, a rock or bottle—something hard—slammed into my mouth.

"I just got hit!" I yelled to Dalio, and I spat out blood and pieces of tooth into my hand. My tongue searched my top row of teeth, finding a front tooth that was now sharp and jagged, while my mouth filled with blood. The car had been sitting in wait for us with its headlights off.

After their direct hit, the kids in the car flashed their lights and screeched off. The windows were low enough now for us to hear their screams of laughter.

We moved to a completely dark area behind some bushes to regroup. Going to the pizza shop was out of the question. Dalio, not panicking, said, "Bro, we have got to get back to campus, now."

I reached into my mouth and wiggled my loose tooth. My mouth was aching. I was beside myself with anger—and still confused. And embarrassed. Embarrassed to have been called a nigger in front of my comrade. And embarrassed by my reaction. Because after being called a nigger and having my teeth broken, I'd decided to flee back to campus. Should I have stayed there in the middle of the street, waiting for the boys to come back, somehow gotten them out of their car, and tested them blow for blow? Part of me was shocked when I decided the answer was no.

I'd only waded into street life in the Bronx; I'd never dived into its deepest, darkest waters. But I'd been around enough street cats to know the code: they hit you with a knife, you find a gun. "Nigger" was the ultimate fighting word. This was the kind of knowledge that was so deeply understood by all it never had to be said out loud.

Still, I knew I had to let this one go. I had to look at the bigger picture. This was not a fair fight. The guys who attacked me were unknown, unnamed, and in a car. If I'd started a fight and won the fight, how would it have ended? And if I'd failed, how would it have ended then? The worst-case scenario was more likely to happen than the best-case scenario.

Dalio and I sat silent for a moment, waiting to see any lights or hear any noise. Then again, as we'd just learned, darkness and silence did not necessarily mean safety.

"We have to get back to campus by a different route. No lights. No streets," Dalio said.

I knew where to go. "Follow me," I said, and I began to run through a series of front yards to a dark, empty field about a quarter mile away. Dalio was trying to ask me where we were going, but I never slowed or turned around to explain. There wasn't time.

Crouching behind trees and cars along the way, we moved closer to our goal. I had thought this uniform gave us security, but here we were, hustling through dirty fields and grassy yards in our black dress shoes and stained wool pants. Our hearts pounded under our navy-blue shirts.

"Where are we?" Dalio asked again when we stopped behind a large rock, staring at the wooded landscape in front of us.

"It's the field that leads us back to school," I replied. This was our chance to get back on campus without having to meet up with our attackers again. Dalio had never been here. Most cadets never had a reason to wind up in these woods. I had, however; in fact, it was one of the first memories I had of this place. This was the same area I'd run through trying to find the Wayne train station, trying to escape.

We bolted into the woods. We navigated the darkness holding on to trees, using the moon as our guide. Minutes later, we saw the light from the cross perched on the chapel's roof, only fifty yards away from our barracks.

The irony of the situation forced me to smile despite my newly cracked tooth. Years earlier, I had run through these same woods with all my might, looking for safety, trying to get away from campus. Tonight, I was running through the same woods looking for safety, in the other direction.

Seven

AIRBORNE

"Five minutes!" the jumpmaster yelled from the front of a C-130 military aircraft.

"Five minutes!" my entire chalk of Airborne candidates yelled back. I stood toward the middle of the C-130, staring at the back of another soldier's helmet. The late-summer Alabama heat beat down through the windows of the airplane we'd been packed into for over an hour. Sweat dripped down my face but, afraid to move, I couldn't wipe it off. One of our instructors—we called them Black Hats—opened the door at the front of the plane and looked out to inspect our drop zone. He braced his hands against either side of the door and stuck his head into the open air, slowly turning from side to side to check for any potential obstacles.

I had gotten used to the fifty pounds of gear strapped to my back, torso, and legs. My bladder was about to explode from the crazy amount of water we were forced to drink to stay hydrated. None of this now mattered. I was about to jump out of a plane. I was eighteen, and I was about to become a paratrooper. I was overwhelmed with excitement and nervousness.

• • •

It had been a little more than a year since I decided to make the army a fundamental part of my future. At the age of seventeen, I was coming to the end of my high school career, and I was starting to get recruited by college programs. I had been a starter on the Valley Forge basketball team since sophomore year. I had a quick first step, a passion for defense, and a decent jump shot. I was making a name on the court, and colleges were starting to notice. I spent my summers at prestigious basketball camps like Five-Star Basketball and Eastern Invitational, camps where college coaches prowl, looking for fresh prospects. The New York Times had even run a two-page article on my high school sports career and future prospects. I was toured around colleges by young and attractive "guides" whose job it was to make me feel welcome—and wanted. At first it made me feel special, as if I were chosen. The girls who admired me added to the allure.

But the attention was starting to make me cocky. I would sit in my room and practice the "grip and grin" to get ready for the day the NBA commissioner announced my name as the Knicks' first-round pick in the NBA draft. I even had some generic lines ready for the interviews I would give to the press:

"Our team works hard, and we play hard."

"My team put its faith in me, and I am just thankful things worked out."

"I believe we can beat any team on any given day, as long as we play our game right."

A few months earlier, Uncle Howard had taken me out to shoot hoops at a park back in the Bronx. I was telling him about how if I kept getting recruitment letters from colleges, I figured it'd only be a matter of time before I could make it to the pros. Howard was still a much stronger player than I was. While I talked about how good I was, he was using his size to post me up down low and then nail a quick turn-around hook shot or layup. His moves reminded me that I wasn't quite in the NBA yet.

After we shot a few more hoops, we talked on the side of the court. "You know, your game is getting pretty good, and I hope you do make it to the league. Then we would all be living nice," Uncle Howard said with a smile on his face. "But you have to understand that the chances are not in your favor. You know how many other kids like you want to be in the NBA? You have to have some backup plans."

I took the ball out of his hands, wanting to practice my midrange jump shot instead of listening to a lecture about my future.

"Think about it, man," he continued. "It's simple math. Only 60 players are chosen in the NBA draft every year.

There are 341 Division One schools, each with 13 players on the roster. This makes 4,433 college players who could declare eligibility for the NBA draft. These numbers don't even include Division Two or Three players. Or international players, for that matter."

"It sounds like you've been practicing this speech for a while," I laughed.

The dose of reality contained in the statistics had bothered me, though, and I hadn't been able to shake it off since that talk.

As I started playing against nationally ranked players at various tournaments and camps, I realized that there were gaps between my talent and theirs. I played hard while other guys played easy, with a gracefulness that I lacked. When you step on the court with players like Kobe Bryant or six-foot-eight point guards who can dunk from the free throw line, you start to wonder if you might be out of your league. Your mind begins to concentrate on your other options.

I realized that Howard was right. I had to make sure colleges knew my name regardless of my game. Just as military school had slowly grown on me, so had academic life. I actually liked reading. My mother had bought me the Mitch Albom book *Fab Five*. The book is about the Michigan basketball team led by Chris Webber, Jalen Rose, and Juwan Howard, a team with five freshman starters who made it all the way to the national championship game. The Fab Five sported baggy shorts, bald heads, and a swagger I recognized from the streets of the Bronx. I loved seeing how the hip-hop generation changed the face of sports, and college basketball in particular. The characters in that book jumped off the page, and I felt myself as gripped by their destiny as I was by my own. I finished *Fab Five* in two days. My mother used it as a hook into a deeper lesson: The written word isn't a chore. It can be a window into new worlds.

From there, I leaped into books with passion. Authors across generations, countries, and races illustrated places in the world I had never been and experiences I had not yet had. F. Scott Fitzgerald, Walt Whitman, and James Baldwin were some of my favorites. Like the hip-hop artists I admired, they brought their hardships alive through creativity, passion, and even humor.

I had spent so much of my childhood feeling out of place. I'd allowed other people to dictate my expectations of myself. I was finally realizing that I could do better than that. I didn't need to have different versions of myself for different people. I didn't have to compromise with white institutions because of my race, and I didn't have to apologize to people in my hometown if I wanted to live a life beyond what was directly in front of me.

Reading gave me a chance to hear about other black Americans' experience with race. I started with *The Autobiography of Malcolm X*, a classic for young black men. Malcolm X insisted that blacks must love their skin and their culture before they can fight racism. I absorbed Malcolm's words, but there was a sense of separation between his reality and mine. The figure who really spoke to my core, though, was the Bronx's own Colin Powell. Both Colin Powell and Malcolm X call for us to change the world. Malcolm X's response to America in the mid-twentieth century was profound and deeply felt, but he didn't speak to my experience the same way Colin Powell did.

Powell's autobiography, *My American Journey*, made me realize how much I needed to understand America's history before I could make my imprint on its present. It also made me certain that I wanted to serve in the army. In his book Powell talked about going to the Woolworth's in Columbus, Georgia, and not being allowed to eat there. African American GIs during World War II had more freedom when they were stationed in Germany than they had back in their own country—the very country they were fighting for. Beginning in the fifties, though, there was less discrimination inside our military posts than in the North *or* the South. Colin Powell could have been angry and given up, but he didn't. He embraced the progress this nation made and the military's role in helping that change to come about. He showed me that the army could help me to love my country, with all its flaws, and to serve her with all my heart.

Powell wanted what I wanted: a fair shot. A chance to develop his talents, and a chance to live them out freely. The problems of race that Malcolm X confronted have not disappeared by any means. But Powell gave me another way to think about the American dilemma and, more than that, another way to think about my own life.

As I started to think about my future beyond basketball,

I wondered what kind of person I wanted to become. How could I become that person? How could I follow in the footsteps of the people who'd had the biggest impact on my life? Aside from my family and my friends, the people I most trusted all had own thing in common: they wore the uniform of the United States of America.

There was my history teacher, Lieutenant Colonel Murnane, who lit a fire in me about the importance of public service and contributing to the communities I lived within. I sat in the front of his class as he spoke about the Constitutional Congress and the Federalist Papers, and their enduring relevance to our existence today.

There was also Colonel Billy Murphy, the commandant of cadets. He was one of the most intimidating but fair people I have ever met. He demanded excellence from every unit, every platoon, and every cadet. He had no interest in excuses—effort and hard work were all that mattered. The last time I saw him was when he made a speech at our chapel. He announced that he was leaving Valley Forge to undergo treatment for advanced-stage cancer. Then he said something I will never forget: "When it is time for you to leave this school, leave your job, or even leave this earth, you make sure you have worked hard to make it matter that you were ever here."

The notion that life is fleeting, that it can come and go quickly and unexpectedly, had been with me since I saw my father die. In the Bronx, the idea that life is not permanent underlies everything. It drove us kids to not even care about our own lives. It stopped us from caring about what happened to us in the future, and it told us not to bother making an effort in the present. Colonel Murphy's speech presented a different point of view.

I learned throughout my life that life's impermanence can be sad and painful. But it is also what makes every single day precious. It's what shapes our time here. It's what makes it so important that not a single moment be wasted. That, I believe, is what Colonel Murphy wanted us to understand.

My next decision became clear over the next few months. I wanted to stay at Valley Forge and attend its junior college. Staying here would allow me to go through the early commissioning process, receive my associate's degree, and become a second lieutenant in the army. I wanted to lead soldiers.

● ● ●

"Three minutes!" the Black Hat yelled enthusiastically.

"Three minutes," we replied, less enthusiastically. I looked around the plane at the faces of my fellow paratroopers. We were a group of soldiers, sailors, airmen, marines, coast guardsmen, cadets. At this moment we were united in how terrified we were. For some, this was the first genuine military activity they were participating in. For a few, this was the first airplane ride they had ever taken. These few, even after today, still wouldn't have had the experience of *landing* in an airplane, just that of taking off—and jumping out.

We tried to hide our trembling legs and shaking hands with broad smiles and nervous laughter. Our sweat-stained uniforms clung to our skin. My left hand grasped the yellow rip cord for dear life as my right hand pressed against the side wall for balance. That bright yellow cord was my lifeline. If it failed, the parachute that was strapped to my belly like a baby kangaroo would be my last hope.

A week before I boarded that C-130 for the most memorable plane ride of my life, Valley Forge had selected me to be the regimental commander for the Seventieth Corps of Cadets. This meant that I would be the highest-ranking cadet in the entire corps of more than seven hundred people. I would be responsible for their training, health, welfare, morale, and success. I remembered watching the regimental commander my first year at Valley Forge with both fear and awe. At his command, the entire corps moved. Wherever he stepped on campus, cadets snapped to attention. Soon I would take on that role.

At eighteen years old, I was the youngest in my group. When I was commissioned, I was told I was one of the youngest officers in the entire United States military. My platoon sergeant would probably be older than my mother. It was one thing leading cadets, but would I honestly be ready at such a young age to lead soldiers? My mind began racing again when a command brought me back to reality.

"One minute!"

"One minute!"

The plane steadied at eighteen hundred feet as we neared our drop zone. In fifteen seconds, my mind replayed three weeks of training. When I landed, I needed to make sure that my feet and knees stayed together, that my eyes stayed focused on an object in the distance—*not* on the ground, I reminded myself—and that my "five points of contact" hit the ground in order (balls of my feet, sides of my calves, hips, lats, and shoulders). It sounds easier than it actually is, I was warned when I first started training. Jumping from a plane the wrong way or landing the wrong way could lead to serious injuries. Even the kinds you can't live to tell the next day.

I concentrated hard. I could do this. Step out with one leg. Chin tight against my chest. Right hand on the handle of my reserve parachute.

Do I count to three or count to four before pulling my reserve?

Which way do I pull my parachute slips if the wind is blowing left to right?

Shoot, I can't remember.

Is that minute up yet?

My mind and my nerves were on edge.

A voice yelling "Get ready, Airborne!" brought me back to task.

Our Black Hats had told us three things to remember when we jumped: "Trust your equipment, trust your training, and trust your God." We were seconds away from taking the leap, and I could feel the prayers in the air. I stared at the yellow light at the front of the plane, waiting for it to turn green. I asked God to watch over me and the others in the plane. Usually I started my prayers with "Dear most heavenly father" and "Most gracious and everlasting God." This time it was just "Help!" and "Please don't let me die like this."

Before I finished praying, the yellow light disappeared and a bright green one lit up right above it.

"Green light *go!*"

The people in front of me shuffled toward the door like commuters leaving a packed subway car. I approached the open door two thousand feet in the air. I'd heard stories about people who, after the Black Hat yelled "Green light go!", had tried to stay in the plane. They were lifted off their feet by the jumpmasters and thrown out. You had to keep the flow of bodies moving in rhythm so everyone landed in the drop zone and not in somebody's yard in the middle of Alabama.

I shuffled toward the door as the line got shorter. My colleagues, I realized, were now flying through the air beneath me. Suddenly, the only person in front of me was the jumpmaster. He stared at me—we were so close that I could see my reflection in his sunglasses. His cheeks were flapping from the wind blowing against his face. I handed him my yellow rip cord, yelled "Airborne, Jumpmaster!" and turned my body to face the open door. I closed my eyes and felt the air just below me whizzing by.

My left leg stepped out over the edge of the doorway. Instantly, I was sucked out of the plane. I heard—no, *felt*—the aircraft speed away. I thrashed around in the wind. It wasn't me who controlled my movements but the rushing air. I refused to open my eyes. I was counting to three in my mind. Then I felt a sudden jerk, and my body was lifted dozens of feet. My parachute had opened.

I opened my eyes. I looked up and, to my relief, saw the canopy above me. It didn't have any holes or tears—it was just sailing above me, letting me glide through the air. Beautiful emotions ran through me: peace, love, appreciation.

I looked down at the trees waving in the distance, and the gorgeous brown Alabama soil that seemed to be rising to meet me. My equipment and training had worked. My faith was confirmed. As I cut through the sky, the wind whipped against my face. I kept my eyes high, staring at the horizon.

I was flying.

Eight
FULL CIRCLE

After settling into junior college at Valley Forge, I met with my college advisor, Miss Pollack.

"Are you familiar with Johns Hopkins University?" she asked me.

Johns Hopkins is in Baltimore. Because I was attending school in Pennsylvania, I didn't live in Baltimore, but I still considered it home. Especially since my mother and sisters had moved back there five years earlier.

So I knew about Johns Hopkins. I knew its medical research center had made some of the greatest medical gifts the world has ever received. Even if it was in the city I knew so well, though, I felt it had very little to do with my life there. It played the same role that Columbia University does for the Harlem residents who surround it, or the University of Chicago does for the South Side. Hopkins made me think of Riverdale. It was full of kids who did not look or sound like me.

"Yes, ma'am. But I don't want to study medicine," I quickly answered her.

"Wes, that's not the only degree they offer!" Miss Pollack assured me. "If you transferred to Johns Hopkins, there would be a lot of options for you. I'd like to arrange for you to meet a friend of mine; he's the assistant director of admissions. His name is Paul White. Just have lunch with him. At the very least, I bet you'll enjoy each other's company."

A week later, I sat across the table from Paul White. I was expecting a heavyset, white-haired gentleman who'd ask for the check the second he heard my SAT scores. What I found was a black man with a warm personality and a booming voice. He was full of energy, gesturing as he spoke to act out what he was saying. I told him my story, and he told me about the school. By the end of our meal, he let me know he thought I would fit in great. I was touched.

But there was still the matter of getting in. My SAT scores were hundreds of points below Johns Hopkins's standards. I may have been a junior college graduate and an army officer, but I knew that landing admission at Hopkins would be a stretch. So after filling out the application and mailing it, I put it out of my mind. But months later, I got the large package in the mail. Not only was I accepted—I'd receive scholarship money. I read the letter aloud to my mother over the phone, and she screamed in excitement.

I beamed. The feeling of making her proud was almost dizzyingly good. I'd spent so much of my life running from her and her discipline. I had been trying to show her I didn't need her as much as she thought. As I got older, she was easing up. Our relationship wasn't just mother-to-son, it was now also friend-to-friend.

I realized that Hopkins represented much more than a chance to attend a top school with a great reputation. It was also my chance to go home. I had been craving it.

● ● ●

"Wes, the mayor will see you now."

As I began walking toward the mahogany door of the mayor's office, I instinctively stuck my hands in my pockets and pushed down, trying to straighten out my pants. For close to a decade I'd dressed in a uniform every day. Now, even after two years of being back in Baltimore, fashion still wasn't my specialty. This was my best blue suit, but it was too small.

"Hey, General, how's everything going?" Mayor Schmoke said as I cautiously entered and shook his hand. "General" was his nickname for me. He was poking fun at the fact that I was a brand-new second lieutenant in the U.S. Army Reserve—which, by the way, is as far from a general as an officer can get. I was on my second internship with the mayor, but he still intimidated me. Every time I stepped into his office, I felt self-conscious. Even his famously toothy grin failed to put me at ease. It was probably because I looked up to him so much.

Kurt Schmoke had been the mayor of Baltimore for

twelve years. The city had changed for the better under his leadership; Baltimore had been named an Empowerment Zone by President Clinton in 1994.

But he was frustrated by how slowly his beloved city was changing. The problems he'd been dealing with for over a decade weren't out of sight. The murder rate had not fallen under three hundred in years. The rate of sexually transmitted diseases had risen sharply, and so had the teen pregnancy rate. Schmoke was a young, photogenic Yale-, Oxford-, and Harvard-educated lawyer, and he had come to learn that the problems of urban America were bigger than he was.

Of course, Baltimore has its rough parts, but to this day it has strengths, history, and opportunity. It's the birthplace of Babe Ruth and Thurgood Marshall, Edgar Allan Poe and Billie Holiday. Francis Scott Key, a lawyer and native Baltimorean, penned "The Star-Spangled Banner" after watching the British bombardment of our new nation's soldiers at Fort McHenry. Baltimore is the home of the B&O Railroad and the best crab cakes anywhere.

However, its also a city that is divided. Almost every other major city in this country leads the same kind of double life. Downtown Baltimore, where the Orioles play and the fancy Inner Harbor lies, is not the whole story. Those who brag about Baltimore often ignore the poorer, grittier areas. Yet these were the areas Mayor Schmoke gave his attention.

He asked me to take a seat on a couch. His office was elegant. Plaques and awards lined the walls, along with photos of the mayor with presidents, prime ministers, and everyday Baltimoreans. The office reflected the man—impressive but down-to-earth.

Mayor Schmoke eased into a chair across from me. He leaned back, rubbing both hands over his thinning hair, and asked me how I had enjoyed my internship.

"I've loved it, sir," I said frankly. But my single-sentence answer didn't even begin to cover the impact being in his office had had on me. I didn't know how to express my gratitude in words.

"What do you plan on doing after you finish school?" he asked next.

I was dreading this question. I really had no idea. Without even thinking, I heard the words "law school" escape from my mouth, I guess because that sounded respectable. I was trying to impress him, but, to my surprise, Mayor Schmoke waved his hand at the idea.

Then he leaned in. "Have you ever heard of the Rhodes Scholarship?"

I had heard of it. I knew it was a fancy academic award. I'd heard that Mayor Schmoke, President Clinton, and our state's senior senator, Paul Sarbanes, were all Rhodes Scholars.

"Let me show you something," he continued, rising from his seat and moving toward the wall. I followed him. He pulled out a pen and pointed to a framed black-and-white picture. He reeled off some names. One of the people in the picture, he noted, was now a writer at the *New Yorker* magazine, and another was a member of the Clinton administration. Then he pointed his pen a few inches over.

"And there I am. This is my Rhodes class."

I stared at the photo of eighty young faces smiling into the camera. The men's plaid suits with large collars, the thick knotted ties, and the bushy mustaches had all obviously been stylish back when he went to Oxford but looked a little funny to my eyes. Then again, my too-small suit didn't exactly qualify me as a fashion critic. I was surprised that I recognized a few other faces in the crowd. This was a group of people that had influence. They had brought about real *change*.

"That was a great time in my life," Mayor Schmoke reminisced. "We'd go to the pub after class and argue over a couple of beers." He laughed. "Respectful arguments. Debates. I was living and studying in buildings constructed hundreds of years before our country was even founded. And Europe was right there at our fingertips. I could travel to a whole other country in the time it takes us here in America to travel to another state."

I nodded, eager for more.

"It's not easy to go to a new country," he said. "It takes courage, and it takes independence to dare to be an outsider. It was an odd feeling to be a minority outside of the United States. I was there not just as a black person in the middle of white people, but as an American in the middle of Europeans."

This was fascinating to me. This was my last day interning

with the mayor. In a week I would be leaving for a semester abroad. I was going to South Africa with a group of four-teen other American students to study at the University of Cape Town. Besides taking classes, we would be learning the language and the culture. I had been outside of America before—I'd visited Jamaica to see family when I was grow-ing up, and I'd been to Cuba on a class trip with a group of Johns Hopkins students. But going to South Africa would be my first long-term trip abroad. I wasn't sure how I would get used to my new surroundings.

Before I left we shook hands. I thanked him for the op-portunity to work with him. As I headed away to the build-ing's archway, he called out, "And, Wes?"

I turned around. "Yes, sir?"

"Apply for a Rhodes Scholarship, would you?"

I wasn't sure what else to say, so I said another "Yes, sir."

"Look up who Cecil Rhodes was. Know his legacy before you apply for his scholarship," he added, before giving me a final nod and disappearing behind his door.

I headed straight to the library to follow the mayor's ad-vice. Cecil Rhodes, I learned, had left an ugly legacy. He was a nineteenth-century businessman who took pride in his greed and his racism. He started the scholarship to en-able white men, and white men only, to get excellent educa-tions. Generations later, this legacy had been turned around for the better. The scholarship could now be used by a per-son like me, someone a racist like Cecil Rhodes would've despised. It made sense that Mayor Schmoke wanted me to learn the history of the scholarship: he wanted me to know that we *can* change the world that Rhodes and people like him had left for us. I remembered Colin Powell's message. The bloody, violent, painful past is important because it is what shaped us. But the future doesn't have to repeat the past.

It turned out that, years ago, Mayor Schmoke had been given the confidence to apply for the Rhodes Scholarship when he'd met Judge Robert Hammerman and Senator Sarbanes of Maryland. Now he was passing the same favor on to me.

I thought about Paul White and how he'd encouraged me to go to Johns Hopkins in the same way two years earlier. Mr. White had gotten to know me and my story on a personal level. Having him rooting for me on the inside had obviously helped me.

As I got older and was able to peer into a wider world, I was disturbed by the way privilege and preference work in the world, and how unfair it could be. So many opportunities in this country are distributed to those who are privileged. The rest of us have to rely on an uncertain mix of chance and hard work. Otherwise, we would keep finding ourselves on the outside of opportunities for power and prestige.

People in my parents' generation were so hopeful during the civil rights movement. They hoped to have a shot, only to have the rug pulled out from under them. From 1981 to 1989, the education budget was cut by half. Students who couldn't afford college relied on scholarships and grants—like Basic Educational Opportunity Grants, known as Pell Grants, or Pells. When politicians stopped funding those grants, students were left without the financial support and they were forced to drop out. They were spun right back to the streets and away from their true ambitions.

Many of the kids I grew up with in the Bronx—including guys like Shea, who lived outside the law—figured that they'd never have a shot at success outside the hood. Then there were some who started out as underdogs and managed to move up. I was lucky to have supportive, encouraging people to help guide me. Hard work is essential, but you also need people around you who believe you can make it. Otherwise, if you don't think you can succeed, what would you bother working for?

It made me think more about the Rhodes Scholarship and Cecil Rhodes's legacy. We can't let the others stay behind like he did. For those of us who are lucky enough to move up, it's our job to pull our brothers and sisters up with us. That's what Mayor Schmoke and Paul White, and many others, did for me.

Nine

WATENDE

A few weeks after my conversation with Mayor Schmoke, I was headed to South Africa. South Africa is below the equator, so the seasons are the opposite of ours in the United States. I got on my plane dressed for an East Coast winter day—a sweater and oversize down jacket. When my flight arrived in Cape Town, South Africa, fifteen hours later, I walked out into the eighty-five-degree heat in a T-shirt, shorts, and sunglasses.

"Are you Wes?" a strongly accented voice shouted toward me. The pronunciation made my name sound like "Wez." It was a strange mix of Australian and Dutch accents, I guessed. A tall, thin, but muscular man was walking toward me in khaki shorts and a Bahama shirt. A pair of sunglasses rested on top of his balding head.

"I am," I cautiously replied.

"I'm Zed, director of the study-abroad program. Zed is a nickname taken from my first initial, Z."

I must have looked confused.

He smiled. "The letter 'Z' is pronounced 'Zed' in most of the English-speaking world outside of the States."

"I never heard that before, but I'll take your word for it," I said, shaking his hand.

I don't know what I was expecting for my introduction to Africa, but it sure wasn't a white man with a funny accent and name.

Zed led me and the fourteen other college students to a van. We unloaded our bags and piled in. Tired and jet-lagged, we all stared out the windows. Some people trailed off to sleep, but I leaned against the window and looked through the glass. I was amazed by the natural beauty of the country. I knew Africa wasn't just a giant safari. My grandfather, who'd worked in Africa as a missionary, would tell me about the tremendous cultural diversity throughout the continent. But I was in no way prepared for the massive skyscrapers and gorgeous beachside drives I saw that first day. I could see the clouds rolling off Table Mountain and the crowds of people strolling down the V&A Waterfront. This city could be dropped onto any American coast and fit right in, I thought.

The group had studied South Africa's complicated history to prepare for the trip. For decades, South Africa had been governed under the rules of apartheid, a government-enforced system of racial hierarchy. So-called nonwhites were *legally* segregated into certain areas. They were forced to live in townships, small towns that had been created for one reason: to isolate black Africans in poverty-stricken areas away from the whites. When police came through the townships, it was to harass the residents, not to protect them. Segregation was enforced strictly and violently under apartheid. Even though this land was infinitely more extreme and more dangerous than where I was from, I couldn't help but think of the broken-down housing projects in the Bronx and Baltimore.

Apartheid was overturned in 1994 after the country's first democratic elections. Nelson Mandela, a heroic activist of the African National Congress, was sworn in as president after having been imprisoned for almost thirty years. Even with a multiracial democracy, the recent past still loomed over South Africa's cities. Now the country was segregated by economic class instead of race. Most black Africans didn't have the money to be considered part of the "upper classes" after decades of enforced poverty, though; only members of white and light-skinned groups did. Even if segregation was no longer legal, the country was still basically divided by race.

We would be living in Langa, which had been South Africa's first black township. When we passed the downtown area and got off the expressway at Langa, everything looked different. The van bounced up and down as the roads below turned from paved highways to streets covered in dirt and potholes. Out the window, there were shacks rolling out as far as the eye could see. The walls of these shacks were like patchwork quilts of wood, aluminum, and metal scraps. The roofs were just propped-up pieces of metal and the curtains were made of torn cloth. These shacks seemed like they had just been thrown together, but they'd been that way for years. Well, some of them, at least. Every few months or so, someone's makeshift cooking stove would flare out of control. The houses were so closely packed together that a whole section of the land would be burned to a crisp before the fire was extinguished. Within days, shacks would be rebuilt and people would go back to life as usual.

I'd thought that I knew what poverty looked like from living in the Bronx and Baltimore. Now I knew how foolish I was: I didn't know anything. Even in West Baltimore we lived like kings compared with this. In these surroundings I felt an overwhelming sense of both guilt and appreciation for the circumstances I had been raised in.

There were dozens of kids lining every street we drove down. They were staring at the vehicle, and they smiled brightly and gave us the thumbs-up as we rolled past, as if they had known us before. It was strange to feel recognized in a place simultaneously so new and so familiar.

A few minutes after entering Langa, we stopped in front of a simple white home in the middle of Mshumpela Street. Zed looked over his shoulder from the driver's seat and grinned. "Wez, this is your stop." I climbed out of the van and grabbed my overstuffed bag, my entire wardrobe for half a year crammed into a forty-pound-capacity Samsonite carry-on. My white Nikes kicked up dust as I walked up to the house. It would be my home for the next six months.

The door creaked open. A short woman with cropped, curled hair, beautifully clear dark skin, and a radiant smile walked out. She was wearing a dress that reminded me of the West African–inspired kente cloth I had seen in the States. The dress had an intricate pattern of black and white, the traditional colors of her tribe, the Xhosa people. Langa was a mainly Xhosa township. The Xhosa were also the tribe of Nelson Mandela and other heroes of the African National Congress.

I smiled and extended my hand to introduce myself. She ignored my hand and immediately wrapped me in her arms. She hugged me as if I were a family member she had not seen in years. "*Molo!*" she exclaimed as our cheeks pushed against each other—*molo* is the Xhosa word for "hello." Her warmth was contagious, and I squeezed her right back. She said I could call her Mama. Once she let go, I noticed her children standing behind her: a son named Zinzi, who was a few years younger than I was, and a daughter named Viwe, who was eight years old. They were waiting to welcome me to their home.

The family made me feel like one of them right away. Zinzi moved toward me, his short, dreadlocked hair spiked up on top of his head. "Hey, *bhuti,* how was the flight?" he said in a deep baritone voice. *Bhuti* is the Xhosa word for "brother." Viwe was shy. She hugged me quickly, then darted back to stand by her mother's hip.

My first week, I spent almost all of my time after class with Zinzi, his friend Simo, and the other Americans I'd come with. I had not yet spent one-on-one time with Mama. One afternoon she asked me to join her for tea in the kitchen. I sat down at the small table where we ate family meals. It was shaky, with pieces of cardboard stuck under the legs to keep it stable.

I wanted to hear about living through apartheid. Our tea turned into a three-hour marathon of storytelling.

"The color dynamic in South Africa is not the same as in where you are from, Wez," Mama said. "You would be considered 'colored'; you are not dark enough to be considered 'black.'"

"What does that mean?" I asked, shocked.

"'Colored' is an idea that was created during the apartheid era. Really it is to further segregate the races—to pit black people against each other. Coloreds receive more privileges than blacks. Not many more, but enough to create tension and anger between the two groups. The lighter your skin was in apartheid South Africa, the better treated you were."

We talked about the music of the apartheid era and how musicians and artists, even more than the politicians and activists, were the ones who told the rest of the world about the country's injustices. I learned about *ubuntu*, Xhosa for "humanity" and "compassion."

Heroes like Nelson Mandela and a thousand other brave fighters had *ubuntu*: they had managed to change their country from apartheid to democracy without shedding blood.

We were on our third cup of tea when Mama began to tell me about her husband and his role as a freedom fighter during apartheid. He and his fellow soldiers were intimidated, arrested, and beaten for disobeying government rules about carrying personal identification cards.

She trembled as she spoke. "The hopelessness my people felt during this time . . . and knowing the whole time that this segregation, this poverty, this depression was being *forced* on us. That we had done nothing to deserve it. We were not *responsible* for it. And yet it was law, we could not escape it."

I had to ask something. "Mama, I am sorry to interrupt you, but I am very confused. After all of this pain and heartache, how are you now able to forgive? You seem so at peace with yourself and your life. How can you move on?"

She gave me an easy half smile and took another sip from her mug.

"Because Mr. Mandela asked us to."

I'd expected more. I'd expected her to tell me that she was still planning her revenge, or the opposite—that she was afraid their weapons were too strong, so there was no use in fighting.

I must have looked confused, reflecting how I was feeling inside. When I didn't say anything, Mama helped me to understand. "Fighting for your convictions is important. But finding peace is even more important. Humanity and compassion are qualities that every human being is capable of having. That common bond must be stronger than any conflict or fear. Knowing when to fight and when to seek peace is wisdom."

The words "revenge will not be sought" suddenly popped into my head. My father had been right. All at once, Watende, my middle name, made perfect sense.

• • •

A few weeks before I was set to return to America, I was walking with Zinzi and Simo from the *kumbi*, or bus station, back to the house. Township life now seemed second nature to me. Kwaito, a South African mix of hip-hop and house music, blared from passing cars. Children kicked soccer balls back and forth on the dirt-covered road, using large rocks as goalposts. Women spoke loudly to one another, carrying bags and baskets in their arms and on their heads. I was beginning to understand the quick "click" sounds of the Xhosa language, and the feel of the street life.

My stride through the Langa streets was slower and less frantic than it had been when I arrived. I was finally feeling at home.

After class, we would always walk around the neighborhoods, talking to girls from the university campus. Sometimes we'd go to the Mama Africa restaurant to grab one of the best steaks I've ever tasted, or watch cricket at a local bar. All of this felt especially sweet during the last days. My nostalgia always seems to kick in at the end of any meaningful experience. I would soon be heading back to the United States, where, in a matter of months, I would be graduating from Johns Hopkins.

Simo looked sideways at us and said, "So both of you are leaving soon? What am I supposed to do then?"

Zinzi was also going away.

Zinzi, now seventeen years old, was preparing to take the same path as generations of Xhosa boys before him. He would be leaving soon to spend four weeks in the bush, where he and dozens of other boys would join a group of elders and learn what it means to be a Xhosa man. Within days of arriving, the young men would be circumcised, their foreskins removed like childish cloaks that were no longer needed. During the weeks it took the circumcision to heal, they would learn about the history of the tribe, the battles they'd fought, the land they protected, the leaders they'd created. The young men would learn about what it means to be a good father and a good husband. They would meditate and pray together, eat together, and heal together.

They would return to their homes as heroes. A large feast would be cooked for them. They would wear all white for the month after returning, symbolizing that a boy had left, but a man had returned. They would be spoken to differently, viewed differently.

I asked Zinzi if he was scared.

"Not really, man, we all have to go through it. Besides, I've seen others go through it, and how much respect they get. It will be fine."

"Yeah, but I can't imagine that whole circumcision thing without any pills, man. Way too painful, if you ask me!"

Zinzi laughed and said, "I hear you, but it's not the process you should focus on; it's the joy you will feel after you go through the process."

I was impressed by how unafraid he sounded.

Back home, I thought, manhood isn't guided or celebrated through a formal ceremony. There's no official passage from childhood to adulthood. In fact, it feels like we enter adulthood almost by accident. Adult-size responsibilities pop up unexpectedly, and it's up to us to take them on. For some, this comes sooner than for others.

Later that evening I was struck by the sight of a young man on the street. From his all-white clothes, I recognized that he must have just finished the ceremony Zinzi was about to begin. He was a teenager but was walking with the dignity of a man double his age. The confidence in his stride was something that Zinzi did not yet have, something that Simo did not yet have. Something that I did not yet have.

Our eyes met, and he smiled and nodded. I nodded respectfully in return.

● ● ●

While I was in South Africa, I got to talk to my mother on the phone. I was excited to share my experiences. I especially wanted to tell her about Mama, whom I knew she would respect immediately. She responded to me with interest, but her voice sounded strange.

"Mom, you sound stressed," I commented. "What's up, is everything okay?"

"Everything's fine, but I have something crazy to tell you. . . . The cops are looking to arrest a guy in your neighborhood, with your name, for killing a cop."

Ten
THE OTHER WES MOORE

I moved to England after college, on a full scholarship to Oxford University. I was the first African American graduate of Johns Hopkins to become a Rhodes Scholar.

Years later, I returned to Baltimore. Soon I was going to start a fellowship at the White House.

I was thrilled. I was also distracted. Somehow I was still thinking of the story I'd first heard from my mother, about the young man who was the same age as me, from the same streets, with the same name. Wes Moore.

When I'd returned from South Africa, my mother had said, "I'm so glad you were away when this all happened. It would've been so easy for you to be picked up by the police."

I followed the case obsessively. It all started with a jewelry store robbery gone terribly wrong. The robbers shot and killed the store's security guard—an off-duty police officer named Bruce Prothero, who was working a second job

to make extra money for his family. Four young men were
charged with the murder. Two of those men were Richard
Antonio Moore and his half brother Wes. They were each
serving a life sentence in jail.

Two years after this terrible tragedy, I was still thinking
about one of the people arrested for the crime, the other
Wes Moore. As time went on I learned we had much more
in common than just our names. As I studied, worked, and
explored some of the most beautiful places our world has to
offer, I imagined him surrounded by the four walls of a prison
cell, trapped until he died. Sometimes in my daydreams, his
face was mine.

I didn't even know this man. Why did I feel such a
connection with him? Why did I feel as though we were
somehow joined, when we'd never met? I worried that I was
being dramatic or self-involved. But still, I couldn't shake
him. Finally, I wrote him a simple letter introducing myself and explaining how I'd heard about him. There were so
many questions running through my head as I wrote, I didn't
even know which ones were appropriate to ask a stranger.
Who are you? I wanted to ask. Do you see your brother?
How do you feel about him? How did this happen? Do you
feel regret? As soon as I mailed the letter, I felt regret. I
was crazy, expecting him to answer a stranger's questions. A
month later, I was surprised to find in my mailbox an enve-
lope stamped with a postmark from the Jessup Correctional
Institution in Maryland. He had written back.

When I learned how much our experiences had

overlapped before we went on our very different paths, it made me think. How was it that he wound up on his path and I on mine? Why wasn't it the other way around?

That was the start of our being pen pals. Soon I began visiting him in prison. Over the years, we became close. We still are. We definitely have our disagreements—and Wes, it should never be forgotten, is in prison for his participation in a heinous crime. However, even if we make bad decisions, even the worst kinds of decisions, we are still human.

Through our letters, conversations, and interviews, I have pieced his life story together. As with most things in life, I realized that the more I learned, the more complicated the story became. It was easy to make assumptions and draw premature conclusions about Wes, his life, his circumstances. I am not making excuses for the tragedy that led to his imprisonment, but I did find that his story, his whole story, shed light on the path he had taken. Here are some of the things I learned.

● ● ●

Wes Moore was six years old the first time he laid eyes on his father, Bernard. Bernard had been drunk. He usually was. Wes's mother, Mary, hadn't seen the man in years. He had all but disappeared by the time Wes was born in 1975. Bernard hadn't found a steady job since dropping out of high school. He was not the kind of man Mary wanted as a partner or as a dad for Wes and her older son, Richard Antonio, or Tony. She figured she was better off raising her sons alone than with someone abusive and alcoholic. She separated from Bernard in an attempt to protect her children.

Wes and Mary ran into Bernard by accident one day. He looked Mary up and down and said, "Hey, girl, . . . you look *good*." He hadn't recognized Wes. To Mary, the fact that Bernard couldn't place Wes's face was not only insulting, it was laughable. Wes looked just like him. Their skin was the same deep brown tint, and they had the same short, even haircut. Bernard had always been loud and liquored up, though, and Wes was quiet and reserved. Wes was always tall for his age, and athletic. He had a grin that stretched across his entire face and had a way of putting everyone at ease. Especially Mary.

Mary got pregnant with Tony when she was fifteen. Her mother, who had also given birth as a teenager, told her, "No matter *what* happens, you are going to finish school and go to college." Their neighborhood in Baltimore City had been practically a war zone since the 1960s riots after the death of Dr. Martin Luther King Jr. Education seemed like Mary's ticket out. She worked hard to have the opportunities her mother regretfully never did. Mary was thrilled when she graduated with honors from Baltimore City Community College and was accepted at the prestigious Johns Hopkins University and awarded a Pell Grant to help her pay for her education there.

Halfway through her progress toward a degree, Mary received a letter that shattered everything she had worked for.

The letter stated that the federal budget for Pell Grants was being slashed. Her grant was over. Without financial aid, she knew she could never afford to finish her degree. She had been working part-time as a secretary. The $6.50 an hour she was making was enough to keep the balance of her tuition paid, the lights on, and the kids fed—as long as her scholarship was in place. She had always explained to Wes and Tony the significance of being the first one in the family to go to college. Now the door was closed on finishing those dreams. She let Johns Hopkins know she was dropping out. That part-time secretary job became permanent.

· · ·

When Wes was eight, Mary had saved enough money for them to move out of the Cherry Hill Homes. In Cherry Hill, half of the eight thousand residents lived below the poverty line, and the playground bustled with drug activity. Mary was glad to get out of there. Their new home was a three-bedroom house in a suburb called Northwood. She felt safe and hopeful amid all the neat houses and grassy lawns.

Wes liked to think of himself as the man of the house because Tony usually stayed with his dad in the Murphy Homes project. Murphy Homes, nicknamed "Murder Homes," was one of the most dangerous projects around. Tony had started dealing drugs before he was ten. By the time he was fourteen, he had a fierce reputation in West Baltimore. Tony had an ice grill that made you think twice before messing with him. An ice grill is the kind of look you *don't* want to get from someone—it'll stop you in your tracks. It's cold as ice, but fiery with anger.

Tony was six years older than Wes. He was Wes's idol. To Wes, he was a certified gangster. Tony wanted to teach his little brother to be tough and proud—to be a fighter like he was. He tried to protect his brother as best as he knew how. Sometimes he would have Wes over to wrestle with his crew at Murphy Homes. He'd tell Wes, "Rule number one—and don't you forget it—is if someone disrespects you, you send a message so fierce that they won't have the chance to do it again." It was Murphy Homes law and Wes took it to heart.

But Tony also wanted Wes *not* to be like him. He wanted his little brother to stay out of trouble and stay clean—away from drugs and guns. Tony never let on, but no matter how tough he was, or how many corners he controlled, what he really wanted was to go back in time, to before he'd gotten himself so deep in the game, and do it all over.

It made him mad that Wes was already doing badly in school.

"Yo, you need to take your education seriously, man," he'd yell. "Acting stupid ain't cool!"

Tony dropped out in eighth grade—how can he tell me to be a good student? Wes wondered. The only times he ever felt irritated by Tony was when Tony lectured him about school.

Wes's test scores were high enough to pass, but he was skating by. He didn't act up, which kept him under the radar.

Wes had always been one of the brightest kids in class, but the work didn't interest him. Besides, football was taking up his concentration now. He was playing defensive end on the Northwood Rams recreation football team. He was a natural player. Wearing the crimson-and-white Northwood jersey gave him a sense of pride and belonging.

Wes's best friend, Woody, was also on the team. Woody came from a working-class, two-parent household. Seeing a family where the father and mother lived together was new to Wes, and he liked it. Besides Woody, Wes's other good friend was Paul, whom everyone called "White Boy." White Boy's father was Lebanese American and his mother was white. Even though they teased him for being one of the few white kids in West Baltimore, they loved him. Wes would always say, "The only thing white about him is his skin. Everything else is black. He's a real black dude." White Boy would just shrug and say, "It's not my fault. I was born this way."

These had been Wes's boys since he'd moved out to Northwood, and they would remain his boys for life.

• • •

Baltimore City had a 70 percent high school dropout rate in 1987. Mary was scared that Wes, now twelve years old, would follow in Tony's footsteps down that track. They had just moved from Northwood to Dundee Village in Baltimore County, where Wes was going to repeat sixth grade at a new school. Mary worked hard and risked a great deal for her kids. But sensing that the city was not the best option for her children, she continued to move farther away in the hope of salvaging her family elsewhere.

One day Wes met a kid on his block wearing a headset straight out of the Janet Jackson "Control" video.

"You wanna get one of these sets?" the kid asked Wes. "All you have to do is this: when you see a jake roll by, you push this button and say something. You get paid after your shift."

It was everything Tony had warned him against. It was the drug game. No matter what position you took, Tony said, drugs were a game for life—you could be in jail or dead in a snap.

I'm not actually *selling* drugs, Wes reasoned. All I'm doing is making a little cash talking into a headset.

Tony was always sporting the newest clothes and gold rope chains that he'd bought with his drug money. Wes was sick of being stuck with the same beat-up Adidas and jerseys. His mother would come back at him hard whenever he complained. "And you see Tony going in and out of the hospital with gunshots," she'd say. "You want that, too? Be thankful for what you've got!" Wes heard his mother, but like so many kids his age, he chose carefully what to listen to. Now Wes would have pocket money to tide him over; at least, that was the initial thought.

Soon the back wall of Wes's room was covered with a tower of sneaker boxes. Inside the boxes were Nikes, in a rainbow assortment, each pair fresher than the last. The barely touched leather filled the room with a new-leather smell. He was dealing now, and money was coming in fast. He told Mary he made money DJ'ing in the neighborhood. Maybe Mary believed him, or maybe she just *wanted* to believe him, because she didn't ask too many questions. Tony knew better.

"There are not enough records to spin, enough beats to play, to buy that many sneakers," Tony said when Wes fed him his DJ story. He was in full-on ice grill mode. He closed his eyes and asked, pounding out every word: "Wes. Where. Did. You. Get. The. Money?"

"I told you, man, I made this money D—" Before Wes finished his sentence, Tony cocked his arm and punched his brother dead in the face. Then Tony pinned him down and punched his face and ribs again and again. Mary broke them apart and demanded to know what was going on.

"Wes is out there hustling! I told him to leave this alone, but he won't listen!" Tony yelled. "You really believe he's DJ'ing? You're serious? Are you blind?"

Wes knew he was disappointing his brother, which hurt much more than the beating he'd just taken. Tony had been trying to keep him in school and away from drugs for as long as he could remember. But Tony was still deep in the game himself! If he couldn't come up with any better plans, how could he expect Wes to?

They were a long way from their days of youthful innocence, and they both felt it right then. Catching lightning bugs in jars, playing freeze tag on the Cherry Hill streets, and going to the Ocean City beach on summer days with their mother—those days were over.

The next day, while Wes was in school, Mary searched his room. "Please let it be DJ'ing money," she prayed. A shoe box under the bed caught her eye. When she slid the lid off, she was faced with piles of pills, marijuana, powdered cocaine, and vials of "ready rock," or crack cocaine.

She felt like she'd been punched in the stomach. It wasn't just the drugs, it was the lying. Her mind raced: Who is to blame for this? Tony, the neighborhood, the school system, Wes's friends?

When Wes came home and saw the shoe box on top of his mattress, he knew he was busted. What could he say? Maybe that he was holding it for a friend. Or that it had been planted in his room by his enemies. He opened it. It was empty. His fear of getting caught turned to anger.

He bounded into Mary's room and shouted, "Ma, what'd you do? Where are the drugs?"

"I flushed them down the toilet," she replied coolly.

"That was over *four thousand dollars* in drugs! I have to pay someone back for that!"

She shook her head and narrowed her eyes. "Not only did you lie to me, but you were selling drugs and keeping them in my house! Putting all of us in danger because of your stupidity. I don't want to hear your sob story about how much money you owe. You are twelve years old! What are you doing with four thousand dollars? You will stop selling that stuff. I will be checking your room, and I don't want to ever see it in here again. Now get out of here."

Wes knew that the amount of money you made was determined by how hard you worked, and how feared you were. He would make sure that the streets got him that money back, and more. The demand for drugs never ran out.

•   •   •

Wes's athletic physique and laid-back style had always made him popular with the girls around town. New sneakers and brand-name clothes gave him even more confidence. Now that he was fifteen years old, he had many girlfriends. One girl especially, Alicia, caught his eye on the high school bus. After school they would head to each other's house, since neither had parents at home during the day.

Within two months of their meeting, Alicia's period was late. Every pregnancy test came back with a plus sign. Wes was dazed. How could they have let Alicia get pregnant? Time went on; Alicia started having morning sickness, her period didn't come, and her belly began to rise. It was undeniable. They were going to be parents.

Wes and Alicia were hardly alone in their predicament. In Baltimore in 1991, 11.7 percent of girls between the ages of fifteen and nineteen had given birth. More than one out of ten.

Wes told Tony, who had just become a father himself. Tony stared at his brother in silence, then cracked up laughing. Mary had given birth a year earlier, making it three sons in the Moore clan, and Tony thought that Wes's having a brother and a son—and a nephew—all about the same age was hysterical.

"This is like a sitcom, man!" Tony declared.

Alicia hoped that she, Wes, and the new baby would become a family. She wanted their child to have the two-parent household that they'd both missed out on.

But Wes didn't want to deal with being a parent. It wasn't that he was worried parenthood would wreck his plans for the future—he didn't really *have* any such plans. It was that he didn't know what the role of "father" even meant. Wes's own father had played zero role in his life. Wes never even thought about him.

Settling down as a family wasn't going to happen. Wes didn't want to stop hustling and he didn't want to stop seeing other girls.

Soon after Alicia gave birth, Wes got himself in a fight that landed him in a juvenile detention facility. It wasn't over drugs. It was over a girl. His latest fling, Melissa, had a boyfriend called Ray. When Ray found her in front of Wes's house, he beat Wes senseless. Wes wasn't even serious about Melissa, but he wasn't going to let Ray get away with stepping up to him. Since he was a kid, Tony's words never left his mind: Send a message. In a rage, Wes grabbed his 9 mm Beretta. He chased Ray through the streets with his gun. Ray hid behind cars and tried to run away. Wes shot at Ray until all sound and movement coming from him stopped.

It turned out that the bullet that entered Ray's shoulder went straight through. No major organs were hit. Because Ray survived, Wes was charged with attempted murder instead of murder. Wes knew he caught a couple of lucky breaks—first for not killing Ray, and second for being put on trial as a minor instead of as an adult.

Wes was released from juvie after six months. When he returned to high school, he knew he wouldn't last long. He was already older than the other kids in his class because of repeating a grade, and now he'd lost a grade being locked up. Teachers were already dealing with overcrowded classrooms. They didn't have the time to teach Wes the basics he'd missed. A lot of his friends had dropped out anyway. White Boy had quit a year earlier and started waiting tables. Woody was one of the only guys Wes knew who had pulled through. Gym was Woody's favorite class. Every other class tied for last place, but he pulled through and passed them all. Wes was proud of him.

But by the end of his tenth-grade year, the drug game became Wes's full-time job. The population of Baltimore was seven hundred thousand, and at least one hundred thousand of those residents were known to be addicts. Dealing was a sure way to make money. Wes had his operation organized with the precision of a military unit or a division of a Fortune 500 company. He liked the feeling of holding down a corner with his boys. It was the place he felt the most in his element. An unbreakable bond united the crew—for many members, it was the only support system they had. It was family.

• • •

After a while, the pressures and dangers of dealing were
starting to outweigh the money. Wes was twenty-one years
old and he was already tired. Tired of being locked up. Tired
of watching drugs destroy entire families, communities, and
the city of Baltimore itself. He was tired of being shot at and
having to attend the funerals of his friends. He and his team
were taking all the risks; they were the ones who faced the
arrests and the danger. His bosses and the connects were the
ones making the *real* money, but they never had to show
their faces on the street. His tolerance was wearing thin. He
needed out. Two events in particular triggered this decision.

For one thing, Wes got caught selling. He'd known right
away that the sell was sketchy. There are a few major tip-
offs that tell dealers something isn't right: if a person looks
unfamiliar or out of place, or doesn't have the lingo down,
the person is probably a cop.

A guy came up to him who wasn't like his usual
customers—the guy had put too much effort into his outfit,
and even the sentence "Do you know where I can pick up
some rock?" didn't roll off his tongue right. Selling to a guy
who put up this many red flags was risky, and Wes knew it
right away. But on second thought, he decided he wanted
the money. He took the risk. In exchange for a small vial of
crack, he took the man's twenty-dollar bill and walked away.
When he turned the street corner, ten cops were there to
greet him. They grabbed him and cuffed his wrists.

Getting arrested was starting to feel routine. Wes wasn't

shocked or afraid anymore, just annoyed. Why him? Why now? He already had enough to worry about.

The other thing that made Wes want to quit dealing was his new girlfriend, Cheryl. He was still in touch with Alicia because they shared two children. His kids with Alicia had come back to back, born in 1992 and 1993; his two new babies with Cheryl came in the same way, born in 1995 and 1996.

He knew Cheryl had done heroin and other drugs in the past. He'd found remnants of drugs in her closet. His love for her and their kids kept him from seeing the truth that was now staring him in the face: Cheryl was not just a person who had tried drugs in the past, she was an addict. The sight of her one day coming off her high, stumbling to the bathroom to vomit, disgusted Wes. He knew this behavior too well; he saw it every day in his customers. It pained him to realize that the mother of his children was an addict, too.

He didn't know what to do. He felt too old to go back to high school. Without a diploma or job training—and with a criminal record—it seemed impossible to find another job to make ends meet. He went to his friend Levy for advice. Levy had managed to get out of the hustling game a few months back. At first, Wes hadn't understood why Levy would give up so much money to go straight. Now he did. He wanted work that was steady and honest. Something that would give him more time with his family without fear of injury, death, or cops.

Levy told Wes about his plan to start Job Corps, a federal

initiative program begun in 1964 to help disadvantaged youth find jobs.

"You live on a campus—"

"Like in prison?" Wes interrupted.

"No, no, it's like a college. And you go to classes that teach you skills for work. I want to land a job as a repairman. They can teach me that. It doesn't even matter that I didn't finish high school," Levy said.

Wes decided to go to the Job Corps interview.

"Do you have a high school degree?" the interviewer asked him.

"No," Wes replied.

She nodded and wrote something on the sheet of paper on her clipboard. "Do you have a record?"

"Yes."

"Are you serious about this program?"

He was. And he realized that the last question she asked was the one that mattered most. Two weeks later, he and Levy caught the bus to the Job Corps campus. The bus was packed with men and women of just about every age. They all had different backgrounds and motivations for being at Job Corps. But they were united in looking for a new chance.

As Wes carried his bags to his dorm, his eyes took in the campus. He had never seen anything like it before. The lawns were green and fresh, and there were basketball courts and volleyball nets up for games. It was far from prisonlike. Even the room he shared with Levy was spacious.

In the first phase of Job Corps, the students took a test.

Then they were placed at the right level of GED (general equivalency diploma) training. Wes finished near the top of his class. He was already reading at the level of a sophomore in college. He completed the course work and received his GED within a month. He was visiting his family in Baltimore City often, and he proudly displayed his new diploma in a frame at home.

Wes's quick success had him thinking differently about his life. He worked on song lyrics in between classes, and thought maybe he really *could* be a rapper. Many of the other students were now looking to him for help with their GED prep, for advice, and for friendship. Just as he had on the street corners of Baltimore, Wes became a leader.

Wes picked carpentry as his professional specialty. He had always been handy. He enjoyed building but was now motivated to learn true skills. Wes's teacher, Mr. Botkin, made him laugh. Mr. Botkin told corny jokes, but Wes appreciated his skill and his commitment to this group of young people whom nobody else seemed to care about.

In class, Wes decided to build a small house for his five-year-old daughter. He wanted it to be big enough for her to get in and play. For much of her life, Wes had been gone—behind bars and now away at Job Corps. The playhouse represented his way of protecting his little girl, sheltering her even when he wasn't there next to her.

Wes graduated from Job Corps in seven months. They were the most important and enjoyable months in his life. The skills he learned and the confidence he gained finally made him feel like he could go in a new direction. He wanted to provide a better life for his kids and make his mother and Tony proud. He wanted to make *himself* proud.

Back in his old hood, the streets seemed the same as when he'd left them seven months earlier. The check-cashing stores instead of banks; the rows of beauty salons, liquor stores, Laundromats, and funeral homes; and the graffitied walls were right where he'd left them. The hood was the hood, no matter how much time passed.

He'd changed, though.

But getting jobs in Baltimore wasn't as easy as he'd hoped. There was temporary work, but nothing stable. For months, he worked ten-hour days to feed and clothe his kids, but when he came home he was too tired to play with them. While at the Job Corps Center, Wes had felt his problems floating off in the country air. Now, already a year after graduating, he realized they had not disappeared—in his absence, they'd piled up. The pressure was breaking him down. Alicia and Cheryl each needed money, and his mother needed more money because she was raising two of Wes's children as well as Tony's kids. Wes must have felt like crying at times, but he'd realized long ago that crying did no good.

If God does exist, he thought, he sure doesn't spend any time in West Baltimore.

Providing for everyone required a job that paid more than nine dollars an hour. He knew he could always make money the fast way—those hundred thousand addicts in

Baltimore were another part of the hood that had stayed right where he'd left them.

Once again, drugs would become his full-time job.

• • •

Mary sat down to watch the news. A local story gripped her attention.

In broad daylight, four masked men had run into J. Brown Jewelers waving guns at the customers, ordering them to the ground. "Keep your hands on the backs of your heads! I ain't playing with you!" one of them shouted.

They ran to the display cases, quickly and decisively pulling out watches and necklaces as if they already knew what they were looking for. All together they took $438,000 worth of watches and jewels. Then they ran out to the parking lot where a getaway car was waiting.

Some of the people in the store raised their heads to watch the men leave. One of them was Sergeant Bruce Prothero, a thirty-five-year-old police officer who had worked in the Baltimore County Police Department for thirteen years. Prothero was working part-time as the jewelry shop's security guard to make extra money. He and his wife needed to support their five children, including triplets. He was supposed to be off that day but was covering the shift for his coworker.

Sergeant Prothero followed his instincts and ran out after the robbers. He was known around the department as a man ferociously devoted to protecting his family and his colleagues. Pulling his weapon from his holster, he sprinted outside to the parking lot. He was creeping toward the getaway car when suddenly a gloved hand pointed a handgun out the window. The gun let off three shots, striking Prothero at point-blank range. As Prothero fell to the ground, the car screeched away.

The day after the shooting, the cops arrested two men found selling the stolen watches. The men each confessed to the robbery but denied pulling any trigger. Two of the robbers who had killed Prothero were still on the loose.

The news reporter wrapped up the story by announcing that the final two suspects were assumed to be "armed and very dangerous." The photos of these suspects filled the TV screen.

Mary's heart broke when she saw the faces of Tony and Wes.

At four o'clock the next morning, the cops showed up at her house to inspect every corner of every room. But she had no idea where her sons were.

Twelve days later, the cops found Wes and Tony in Philadelphia. They were staying with an uncle who lived there.

Word of the arrest spread quickly through the Baltimore City and Baltimore County police departments. The newspapers and television networks ran nonstop coverage of the arrest. The cops rejoiced. They took this case personally: Prothero had been one of their own.

At home, Mary wept.

• • •

A year after the arrests, Tony and two other defendants were found guilty for the robbery and sentenced to life in prison without parole. Tony was charged as the shooter; he avoided a possible death sentence by pleading guilty to felony murder.

Wes, now twenty-four, took his case to trial. He insisted that he had not been there the day of the murder.

Witnesses were called and videotapes were shown. A saleswoman at the jewelry store testified that she recognized Wes as one of the four men who'd robbed the store. A necklace that was found at the scene of the crime had his DNA on it. The defense attorney claimed the police were harassing people in the neighborhood, trying to drum up even shaky evidence and confessions.

The prosecution asked, "Why would he have fled to Philadelphia right after the murder if he hadn't been trying to escape the police?" Wes said he took the trip without even asking his brother why they were leaving Baltimore.

Now Wes was moments away from finding out which story the court would believe. He looked at the six men and six women of the jury, but no one looked back. He felt very alone. He knew what the foreman was going to say before the man even parted his lips. Wes stared straight ahead.

"On the charge of first-degree felony murder, the jury finds the defendant . . . guilty."

Wes's sentence would be the same as that of the other

three. He would spend the rest of his life in prison without the possibility of parole.

"You committed an act like something out of the Wild West, and you didn't even realize how outrageous it was," the judge said from his platform. "That makes you a very dangerous person."

The widow of Sergeant Prothero hugged her father and sobbed. About ten feet away, Wes's mother, his aunt, and Alicia sat stunned with tears in their eyes. Wes kept his eyes fixed on the front of the courtroom, never once looking behind him to see the Prothero family or even his own. He winced as the familiar cuffs closed around his wrists and a large guard began to walk him out of the room.

Wes and his boys had been in and out of jail since they were adolescents.

But he'd never seen this coming.

Maybe because it's almost impossible to tell the difference between second chances and last chances.

Or maybe because he'd never thought ahead about his life at all. He'd always figured that to get by in the hood, short-term plans were enough. Now, all of a sudden, Wes's future was sealed.

Eleven
THE RETURN

Now you see that this story is about these two boys with similar backgrounds and an identical name: Wes Moore. But I hope that just as this story ended up representing much more to me as I wrote it, it will mean much more to you. Because when we try to better understand individual stories, it is amazing how thin those lines can be between our life and another life altogether.

Compiling this account has taken hundreds of hours of interviews with my friends and family, as well as with Wes and his friends and family. Some names have been changed to protect people's identities and the quiet lives they now choose to lead. The process of tracking down these people and listening to their stories has been one of the most interesting experiences of my life. These folks have shared some of the funniest, saddest, and most thought-provoking real-life tales I've ever heard.

For over two years, my days would begin at five-thirty in the morning, and a cup of tea later I would be in front of my computer, taking my notes and research and trying to piece them into a coherent story about these two very real lives. My father was a journalist, and I hope that in putting all this information together I have echoed his passion for getting the story right. It's been eye-opening, because when you start your day reading letters from someone who will spend the rest of his life in prison, or by reading articles about a police officer and father of five who went to work one day and did not come home, your life and problems are put into a different perspective.

It's been years since my first letter to Wes. I have grown significantly since getting to know him; I'm sure he would acknowledge that he has grown as well. Some people have asked why I am still in touch with him. Why we still communicate. I understand people's concerns, and let me be clear: the only victims on February 7, 2000, were Sergeant Bruce Prothero and his family. I have never tried to make excuses or create sympathy for Wes. But even the worst decisions we make don't necessarily remove us from the circle of humanity. His story deserves to be heard. Not because it is exciting or should be emulated, but because there is so much to learn from it. I didn't reach out to Wes just so I could write a book, so I don't understand why I would stop reaching out to him now that the book has been written.

Besides, despite our deepening relationship, it is impossible for me to become comfortable with or forget where he is. Every time you visit a maximum security facility, you are surrounded by reminders of where you are.

The first time I visited, though, the reality of his environment was particularly striking. The words "Jessup Correctional Institution" were written in bloodred paint on the steel front doors. I stood in front of those doors, pausing before my hand touched the knob. I felt, with a twinge of guilt, how blessed I was to be able to simply walk around in the fresh air. As I paused I savored the feeling; just standing in front of the prison made me aware that my freedom was a miracle, a stroke of incredible luck that I usually didn't think twice about. I could move, explore, meet new people, and simply enjoy the sun beating down on my face.

I took a deep breath and looked around before going into that windowless building.

An armed guard searched and questioned each visitor. The questions were the same every time:

"What is your relation to the inmate?"

"Do you have any electronic equipment or sharp items?"

"Do you have any items you plan on passing to the inmate?"

Soon I was led into a visitors' room as large as a school cafeteria. There were long tables with low metal dividers to separate the visitors from the visited. Armed guards paced from wall to wall, watching with hawk eyes. It seemed like they never blinked.

All around me, reunions were taking place. One inmate, a young man in his early twenties, sat across from a woman with a baby squirming in her arms—he was apparently meeting his child for the first time. Another inmate listened wide-eyed as his grandmother ran down a list of his friends from the neighborhood, updating him on what they'd been up to since he'd gone away. He hung on her every word.

I didn't want to intrude, but I was enthralled by the intimacy of their interactions. I observed them out of the corner of my eye until a guard led Wes to the seat in front of mine.

Initially the conversations with Wes felt uncomfortable, like we weren't sure what we should say to each other. But that dissipated pretty quickly. Quiet uncertainty turned into an almost therapeutic honesty.

"Do you ever think about how things would have been if, say, your dad had been around?" I asked, leaning toward him as much as the partition between us would allow.

"No. I don't think about him at all," he said with a shrug.

"Are you serious?" I asked.

"Yeah. I don't see why you're so surprised," he said, almost amused. "Look. Your father wasn't there for you because he couldn't be. My father wasn't there because he chose not to be. We're going to mourn their absence in different ways. So tell me, what impact did your father's absence have on your childhood?"

"I'm not sure," I said, pausing to think. The major part of my life has been without him. Not having him around was something that always pained me, but I was also used to it. I was lucky to feel the presence of strong women. "My mother took on the role of both parents. I guess both of ours did. But I did always feel my father's absence, yes."

"You still miss him?" Wes asked me.

"Every day. All the time," I replied softly. "He was the kind of man I wanted to be." I was having trouble finding my voice. Thinking about my father always amazed me, because how could I love someone I barely knew so deeply, so intensely?

"When did you feel like you'd become a man?" Wes asked, a troubled look on his face.

"I think it was when I first felt accountable to people other than myself. When I first cared that my actions mattered to people other than just me."

Where did I get off, answering so confidently on that one? I wanted my answer to be as straightforward as that, but I knew it wasn't. This wasn't a job interview. I didn't have to sound perfect or put-together. I could be frank with Wes.

"To be honest," I said, exhaling, "when I started taking responsibility for my behavior, I realized that I had been making a lot of mistakes. When I started to learn from these mistakes . . . I think that's when I became a man. I think when I started appreciating and respecting the things that shaped me instead of turning against them."

"What are the things that 'shaped' you?" he asked, challenging me to draw my answer out.

"I think my environment is what shaped me. The people who raised me. The circumstances I was brought up in— good and bad. What do you think?"

He paused. I waited.

"Well, I agree with you, of course," he said. "But I think it's more complicated than that. I think, above all, we are shaped by our expectations. You and I came from the same areas, so it's not so easy to simply say environment. But other people's expectations of us matter, too, even if we don't want them to. We will wind up doing what they expect us to."

He paused again.

"If they expect us to graduate," he went on, "we will graduate. If they expect us to get a job, we will get a job. If they expect us to go to jail, then that's where we will end up." He gestured around himself with an ironic smile. "At some point you lose control, no matter how much you learn."

As I listened to him, I sympathized, but I wasn't sure I agreed entirely. It sounded like he was saying he wasn't responsible for his actions. As if they were predetermined, like fate, by those around him.

I was reminded, as I frequently am, that Wes is not, by any stretch of the imagination, a dumb guy. He has made some terrible decisions in life, but to me one of the tragedies of this situation is how because of his choices, society was deprived of someone who could have made a valuable contribution.

A guard came over to us. Our time was up. Wes didn't look back as he was led away. I walked toward the exit. Whenever those meetings ended, I found myself leaving with more questions than I'd come in with.

The world outside Wes's prison cell hasn't stopped

changing since his incarceration. In 2008, Wes and his fellow inmates celebrated when Barack Obama won the presidential election, but their enthusiasm faded quickly. They realized that even something as incredible as having a black American president in office could not change their fates.

Wes has also found faith and become a devout Muslim in prison. He started going to mosque services because they were the only opportunity he had to see Tony. Every Friday they have services, and eventually he started to pay attention to the message. His faith has helped him through his time in jail.

Wes loves visits from his children and his mother, Mary, but they're never long enough. Mary is raising two of Wes's children, along with her own nephew and niece, and her youngest son. Wes became a grandfather at the age of thirty-three, during his tenth year in prison. It pains him to have so little time with his family. He has to settle for hearing about their lives instead of participating in them.

Wes doesn't like answering questions like "How are you? What are you up to?" because his days are all the same. He works as a carpenter, making desks and tables, and sometimes he makes license plates. He has two hours of free time a day, "outside time," to play basketball or talk to other inmates. Guards tell him when to wake up, when to eat, and when to go to the bathroom.

So we talk about the past. We talk about how things used to be and how things got to be the way they are.

wes moore

• • •

The past decade has unfolded in ways I never expected it to as a kid.

Since graduating from college, I've worked in a lot of different kinds of jobs. Experimenting with careers has made me realize something: if you always try to follow the path other people lay out for you, you will never excel. Following your passion and your heart is important. But hard work and putting in the effort to be good at something matters. Just like my childhood heroes in the NBA, I realized that I had to work and practice at the things I was passionate about if I wanted to have the kinds of talents that could bring on success.

I have also learned how important it is to share stories, even our own. Statistics provide background. Stories promote action. I wanted to make sure this book was not simply one people would pick up and say "Cool hook." I wanted it to be a call to action. I wanted it to make people feel they could be part of something bigger than themselves.

I have continued to travel around America and the world, speaking with and learning from people about my story and Wes's, and also about their own stories. My favorite part about this journey has been hearing from audiences. People tell me about the versions of each Wes they've known, or even the Wes they've been themselves. The question that still comes up the most is the one that made me want to write this book in the first place: "What was the thing that made the difference between you and the other Wes Moore?" And the truth is that I don't know. It is never that simple. Why did the lives of two people with similar beginnings diverge so drastically? Why did he go one way and I go another? The answer is not something I can fully grasp, and that is because there is no one thing. Our lives and our selves depend on an unpredictable mix of genetics, environments, and straight-up luck. Family lineage matters, education matters, environment matters, high expectations matter. What captured my attention about Wes's story in those newspaper articles at first was simply the name. It was the other details that kept me and refused to let me let go. I did learn, though, the chilling truth that Wes's story could have been mine; the tragedy is that my story could have been his.

According to the national nonprofit group America's Promise, the way many governors decide the number of beds they need for prison facilities is by examining the reading scores of third graders. Elected officials have figured out that kids reading below their grade level by third grade wind up in jail when they get older.

My reading skills in the third grade were far below where they should have been. According to these statistics, I could have been destined for a bed in a correctional facility. I felt handcuffs on my wrists at eleven years old. I began picking and choosing which days were worthwhile to go to school before I even hit my teenage years. I am not proud of many of the things I have done. I disappointed people in ways that still embarrass me. I hurt people who did nothing wrong.

I embraced stereotypes, and I gave people who were really rooting for me a reason to give up. But there were people who saw positive things in me that I didn't even see in myself, and I am thankful for them. Teachers, mentors, ministers, family members, and everyday citizens who cared for my family and me just when we needed it most. I was given a chance to fight the harrowing statistics that surround kids who grow up like me. Through my own experiences, I've become convinced that you have the potential to control your own life, even if the odds are against you.

Learning the details of Wes's story helped me understand my life and my choices, and I like to think that my story helped him understand his. Ultimately, our experiences shed some light on a whole generation of young men: kids like us who came of age in a chaotic and violent time.

In this book, I wanted to figure out what lessons our stories could offer to the *next* generation. Today's young men and women will wind up at some of the same crossroads Wes and I did. Wes agreed to share his experiences in this book so that others could learn from his story and choose a different way. I wanted to tell my own story for a similar reason. I hope that by reading this you can learn from both our failures and our successes.

Adulthood can pounce on you all of a sudden, especially if you're growing up in some of the roughest cities in America. Suddenly you find yourself entrusted with responsibilities that force you to get serious about your behavior. Some of us are forced to carry the burden of others. At the age of sixteen, my friend Justin was left in charge of his dying mother. Wes's mother, Mary, was caring for a baby at the same young age. Others have the opposite situation: they are alone, left to fend for themselves.

From an early age, I was crushed by my father's death. I had wanted him to be there to guide me and to shape me into the kind of man he was. It took me years to realize that in many ways he *did* shape me. I became a man, despite his absence. In fact, his absence made me grow up fast. When he died, my family and I couldn't just fall apart. There wasn't anything we could do to change what happened; we were left to cope with it. I had to toughen up young—we all did, for the sake of the family.

Along the way, I've made mistakes. There are times when I've been irresponsible and ungrateful. I've been so insecure that I felt as if I were an outline of myself for other people to fill in. I haven't always known which battles are worth a fight and which I should ignore. But I've had the freedom to make those mistakes, and the freedom to seek redemption for them.

Sometimes it seems like the world doesn't exist outside your city, your home, your room, even your own head. You may make decisions based on what you see around you; you may follow in the footsteps of whichever role models are available.

A stumble down the wrong path or a shy step down the right one can start up a new, surprising journey. It's both exciting and disturbing to realize that a single choice can give you another life altogether. How do you know which choices are the "right" ones?

It takes practice. It takes patience. It takes people to show you the way. It's asking a lot of yourself to try to "make it" completely on your own.

The most important thing that happened to me was not being physically transported—the moves from Baltimore to the Bronx to Valley Forge didn't change my way of thinking. You take yourself with you everywhere you go. What changed was that I realized how blessed I was to be surrounded with people who supported and encouraged me to work hard and succeed. Sometimes I didn't see them. Sometimes I didn't recognize them. But I know that my best decisions have been made when I took input and advice from people I really respected and admired.

It started with my mom, grandparents, uncles, and aunts, but it led to a string of role models and mentors in military school, in college, and finally in my career. They all kept pushing me to see more than what was directly in front of me. With their help, I could finally see the boundless possibilities of the wider world. Even the unexplored possibilities within myself.

It turned out that I didn't need to let other people's low expectations form me. I didn't need to become a part of a negative statistic. My heroes told me: When people think they have you figured out, prove them wrong. Direct the energy you get from frustration and anger into your own projects, creativity, and, hopefully, success.

I think the best we adults can do for young people is give

you a chance to make the best decisions possible by providing the information, the tools, and the support you need to see the positive in yourself. No matter what your circumstances are.

My people taught me that being black or relatively poor or fatherless, being from Baltimore or the Bronx, would never define or limit me. In other words, they helped me to discover what it means to be free. My only wish—and I know Wes feels the same—is that the young men and women who come after us will know this same freedom. It's up to us, all of us, to make a way for each other.

ACKNOWLEDGMENTS

I first want to thank God. Without his love, forgiveness, and support, I would be nothing.

I remember when I first brought up the idea of writing a book to my wife. I was afraid she would think it was crazy. She didn't. Her support helped ignite the plan, and I am truly grateful. Many of the mornings of writing and editing were done with my daughter in my lap. Even at four months old, she was willing to listen to me rant and read and reread section after section. She was my first reviewer and is my greatest joy.

My entire family has been invaluable throughout this process. From mom, sisters, brothers-in-law, grandparents, uncles, aunts, and cousins to mentors and friends, you have enveloped me in a love that is not just undeniable but heart-warming. I am eternally grateful and humbled beyond belief. Our "family" is more than a family. It's our foundation.

acknowledgments

Linda Loewenthal, once again you served as not just agent but guide. I am and will always be thankful for you. Beverly Horowitz, Rebecca Gudelis, and the entire Random House team have been remarkable to work with. You are committed not simply to sharing books but to changing lives. I applaud and appreciate that. Erica Moroz, thanks for your talents and support.

There are countless others who deserve to be thanked, but that list would literally be an entire new book in itself. You all know who you are, and you know what you mean to me. Bless you and thank you. I am who I am because of you.

Finally, I want to acknowledge all those young people whose stories have inspired me. Young people who far too early have to feel the depths of adulthood. Young people who through no fault of their own have had to take on adult responsibilities. Young people who understand that it's not all about them and who have devoted at least part of their lives to helping others. Please know that you have touched me, as I hope this story touches you.

Resources

ORGANIZATION	SERVICES PROVIDED TARGETING YOUTH	CONTACT INFORMATION
The ACE Mentor Program of America, Inc.	ACE's mission is to inform high school students of career opportunities in architecture, construction, and engineering, and to provide scholarship opportunities.	400 Main St., Suite 600 Stamford, CT 06901 Phone: (203) 323-0020 acementor.org
Action for Healthy Kids	Action for Healthy Kids is committed to engaging diverse organizations, leaders, and volunteers in programs that foster sound nutrition and physical activity in schools.	600 West Van Buren St., Suite 720 Chicago, IL 60607 Toll-Free: (800) 416-5136 ActionforHealthyKids.org
Alpha Phi Alpha Fraternity	This fraternity is committed to the development and mentoring of youths and providing service and advocacy for the African American community.	2313 Saint Paul St. Baltimore, MD 21218-5211 Phone: (410) 554-0040 alpha-phi-alpha.com

resources

ORGANIZATION	SERVICES PROVIDED TARGETING YOUTH	CONTACT INFORMATION
Banking on Our Future (BOOF)	Operation HOPE, Inc.'s, BOOF provides on-the-ground and online financial literacy programs that teach children basic money skills.	HOPE Global Headquarters 707 Wilshire Blvd., 30th Floor Los Angeles, CA 90017 Phone: (213) 891-2900 Toll-Free: (877) 592-HOPE (4673) bankingonourfuture.org
Big Brothers Big Sisters of America	Big Brothers Big Sisters of America helps men have positive mentoring experiences with children, while at the same time giving back to the community.	230 North 13th St. Philadelphia, PA 19107 Phone: (215) 567-7000 bbbs.org
The Black Star Project	The Black Star Project seeks to increase the involvement of fathers and other positive male role models of color in the educational lives of children.	3509 South Martin Luther King Dr., Suite 2B Chicago, IL 60653 Phone: (773) 285-9600 blackstarproject.org
Boy Scouts of America National Council	The BSA provides a program for young people that builds character, trains them in the responsibilities of citizenship, and develops their personal fitness.	scouting.org
Boys and Girls Clubs of America	This organization seeks to inspire and enable all young people to realize their full potential as productive, responsible, and caring citizens.	1275 Peachtree St., NE Atlanta, GA 30309-3506 Phone: (404) 487-5700 bgca.org

ORGANIZATION	SERVICES PROVIDED TARGETING YOUTH	CONTACT INFORMATION
Boys Hope Girls Hope	Boys Hope Girls Hope helps academically capable and motivated children in need to meet their full potential by providing value-centered, familylike homes, opportunities, and education through college.	12120 Bridgeton Square Dr. Bridgeton, MO 63044 Phone: (314) 298-1250 Toll-Free: (877) 878-HOPE (4673) boyshopegirlshope.org
Boys Town	Boys Town provides a beacon of hope for America's children and families through its life-changing youth and health-care programs across the United States.	Toll-Free National Hotline: (800) 448-3000 boystown.org
Children's Defense Fund (CDF) Freedom Schools	The CDF Freedom Schools program partners with community-based organizations to provide free summer and after-school care.	25 E St., NW Washington, DC 20001 Toll-Free: (800) CDF (233)-1200 childrensdefense.org
Children's Health Fund	Children's Health Fund is committed to providing health care to the nation's most medically underserved children.	215 West 125th St., Suite 301 New York, NY 10027 Phone: (212) 535-9400 childrenshealthfund.org
The Coalition of Schools Educating Boys of Color (COSEBOC)	COSEBOC promotes and supports schools determined to make success an attainable goal for all of their male students of color.	281 Summer St., 5th Floor Boston, MA 02110 Phone: (855) 267-3262 coseboc.org

ORGANIZATION	SERVICES PROVIDED TARGETING YOUTH	CONTACT INFORMATION
Concerned Black Men (CBM)	CBM provides youth development services to children from disadvantaged communities.	1313 L St., NW, Suite 111 Washington, DC 20005 Phone: (202) 783-6119 Toll-Free: (888) 395-7816 cbmnational.org
Daddy's Promise	Daddy's Promise was founded to focus the attention of the African American community on the positive relationship that can and should exist between fathers and daughters.	daddyspromise.com
4-H	4-H empowers youths to reach their full potential, working and learning in partnership with caring adults.	4-H National Headquarters National Institute of Food and Agriculture United States Department of Agriculture 1400 Independence Ave., SW, Stop 2225 Washington, DC 20250-2225 Phone: (202) 401-4114 4-h.org
Hip Hop 4 Life	Hip Hop 4 Life is dedicated to empowering young people to adopt a healthy lifestyle. Hip Hop 4 Life serves young people ages ten through eighteen, with a special emphasis on at-risk and low-income youths.	5 Penn Plaza, Suite 1960 New York, NY 10011 Phone: (646) 706-7370 hiphop4lifeonline.com

ORGANIZATION	SERVICES PROVIDED TARGETING YOUTH	CONTACT INFORMATION
A Home Within	A Home Within seeks to heal the chronic loss experienced by foster children by promoting relationships with other current and former foster youths.	2500 18th St. San Francisco, CA 94110 Toll-Free: (888) 898-2AHW (2249) ahomewithin.org
Jackie Robinson Foundation	The Jackie Robinson Foundation serves as an advocate for young people with the greatest need and offers an extensive mentoring program and summer internships.	One Hudson Square 75 Varick St., 2nd Floor New York, NY 10013-1917 Phone: (212) 290-8600 jackierobinson.org
Jumpstart	Jumpstart brings college students and community volunteers together with preschool children in low-income communities for individualized mentoring and tutoring.	308 Congress St., 6th Floor Boston, MA 02210 Phone: (617) 542-5867 jstart.org
Junior Achievement	JA teaches children how they can impact the world around them as individuals, workers, and consumers.	1 Education Way Colorado Springs, CO 80906 Phone: (719) 540-8000 ja.org
The Links, Incorporated	The Links, Incorporated, has a six-decade tradition of mentoring and preparing black children for a bright future.	1200 Massachusetts Ave., NW Washington, DC 20005 Phone: (202) 842-8686 linksinc.org
MAD DADS	MAD DADS patrol city streets to identify unsupervised youths and draw them into program activities.	P.O. Box 22704 Alexandria, VA 22304 maddads.com

resources

ORGANIZATION	SERVICES PROVIDED TARGETING YOUTH	CONTACT INFORMATION
Management Leadership for Tomorrow (MLT)	MLT has made groundbreaking progress in developing the next generation of African American, Hispanic, and Native American leaders in major corporations and nonprofit organizations.	15 Maiden Lane, Suite 900 New York, NY 10038 Phone: (212) 736-3411 Toll-Free: (888) 686-1993 ml4t.org
MENTOR/National Mentoring Partnership	MENTOR believes that, with the help and guidance of an adult mentor, each child can discover how to unlock his or her potential.	1600 Duke St., 2nd Floor Alexandria, VA 22314 Phone: (703) 224-2200 mentoring.org
National Alliance of African American Athletes	The goal of the National Alliance of African American Athletes is to empower young men through athletics, education, and public programs.	P.O. Box 60743 Harrisburg, PA 17106-0743 Phone: (717) 234-6352 naaaa.com
National CARES Mentoring Movement	This organization promotes the mobilization of African Americans to take the lead in fulfilling society's spiritual and social responsibility to children.	408 West 58th St. New York, NY 10019 Toll-Free: (888) 990-IMIN (4646) caresmentoring.com
National Center for Global Engagement	The NCGE is a nonprofit social venture established to create international study, service, and work opportunities for promising American students of color by providing scholarships for study abroad, foreign language training, and meaningful professional development and civic engagement experiences.	1220 19th St., NW, Suite 610 Washington, DC 20036 Phone: (240) 305-5865 nc4ge.org

ORGANIZATION	SERVICES PROVIDED TARGETING YOUTH	CONTACT INFORMATION
National Safe Place	National Safe Place provides access to immediate help for young people in crisis through a network of sites sustained by qualified agencies, trained volunteers, and businesses.	2411 Bowman Ave. Louisville, KY 40217 Phone: (502) 635-3660 nationalsafeplace.org
National Urban League (NUL)	NUL serves as a convening and national partner with the National CARES Mentoring Movement in its attempt to galvanize millions of committed, conscientious, and capable mentors to support today's youths.	120 Wall St. New York, NY 10005 Phone: (212) 558-5300 nul.org
National Urban Technology Center, Inc. (Urban Tech)	Urban Tech aims to provide access to technology and training to address the widening computer literacy and achievement gap in inner-city communities through its two flagship programs, SeedTech and the Youth Leadership Academy (YLA).	80 Maiden Lane, Suite 606 New York, NY 10038 Toll-Free: (800) 998-3212 urbantech.org
Network for Teaching Entrepreneurship (NFTE)	NFTE provides entrepreneurship education programs to young people from low-income communities.	120 Wall St., 18th Floor New York, NY 10005 Phone: (212) 232-3333 Toll-Free: (800) FOR-NFTE (367-6383) nfte.com

ORGANIZATION	SERVICES PROVIDED TARGETING YOUTH	CONTACT INFORMATION
100 Black Men of America, Inc.	The mission of the 100 Black Men of America, Inc., is to improve the quality of life in the black community and enhance educational and economic opportunities for all African Americans.	141 Auburn Ave. Atlanta, GA 30303 Phone: (404) 688-5100 100blackmen.org
Operation HOPE	Operation HOPE is America's first nonprofit social investment bank and a national provider of financial literacy and economic empowerment programs free of charge.	707 Wilshire Blvd., 30th Floor Los Angeles, CA 90017 Phone: (213) 891-2900 Toll-Free: (877) 592-HOPE (4673) operationhope.org
The Panasonic Foundation	The Panasonic Foundation aims to improve public education in the United States.	3 Panasonic Way, 2I-1 Secaucus, NJ 07094 Phone: (201) 392-4132 panasonic.com/meca/ foundation
Raising Him Alone	The Raising Him Alone Campaign is committed to increasing advocacy for single mothers raising boys.	National Raising Him Alone/Urban Leadership Institute 1111 Park Ave., Suite L-151 Baltimore, MD 21201 Toll-Free: (877) 339-4300 raisinghimalone.com
Steve Harvey Foundation	The mission of the Steve Harvey Foundation is to improve public schools in urban areas by upgrading facilities and providing educational and mentoring opportunities.	P.O. Box 52817 Atlanta, GA 30355 steveharveyfoundation.com

ORGANIZATION	SERVICES PROVIDED TARGETING YOUTH	CONTACT INFORMATION
Tavis Smiley Foundation	The Tavis Smiley Foundation aims to develop a cadre of young leaders with critical thinking skills who will share their knowledge and abilities and make a positive impact on the world.	4434 Crenshaw Blvd. Los Angeles, CA 90043 Phone: (323) 290-1888 youthtoleaders.org
TERC	TERC is an education research and development organization dedicated to improving mathematics, science, and technology teaching and learning.	2067 Massachusetts Ave. Cambridge, MA 02140 Phone: (617) 547-0430 terc.edu
United Negro College Fund (UNCF)	UNCF is the nation's most comprehensive higher education assistance organization for students of color. UNCF provides scholarships and internships for students, as well as faculty and administrative professional training.	8260 Willow Oaks Corporate Dr. P.O. Box 10444 Fairfax, VA 22031-8044 uncf.org
United Way Worldwide	The United Way mobilizes millions to give, advocate, and volunteer to improve the conditions in which they live.	701 N. Fairfax St. Alexandria, VA 22314 Phone: (703) 836-7112 worldwide.unitedway.org
WorldofMoney.org (WoM)	WoM is focused on improving the financial literacy of underserved youths ages twelve through eighteen through workshops designed to help students become financially responsible.	1515 Broadway, 11th Floor New York, NY 10036 Toll-Free: (888) 945-8333 worldofmoney.org

resources

ORGANIZATION	SERVICES PROVIDED TARGETING YOUTH	CONTACT INFORMATION
YMCA	YMCA facilities across the nation promote healthy living and social responsibility.	YMCA of the USA 101 North Wacker Dr. Chicago, IL 60606 Toll-Free: (800) 872-9622 ymca.net
Young People's Project (YPP)	The mission of YPP is to use math literacy as a tool to encourage young leaders to radically change the quality of education and life in their communities.	99 Bishop Allen Dr. Cambridge, MA 02139 Phone: (617) 354-8991 typp.org

About the Author

WES MOORE is a graduate of Johns Hopkins University and was a Rhodes Scholar. He served as a paratrooper and captain in the U.S. Army in Afghanistan and as a White House Fellow in the U.S. Department of State. He was named one of the top young business leaders in America and has appeared on the cover of *Time* magazine, which featured him in the article "The New Greatest Generation." Wes lives in Baltimore with his wife and daughter.